Editors
Kim Fields
Heather Douglas

Managing Editor
Ina Massler Levin, M.A.

Illustrator
Mark Mason

Cover Artist
Tony Carrillo

Art Production Manager
Kevin Barnes

Imaging
James Edward Grace
Craig Gunnell

Publisher
Mary D. Smith, M.S. Ed.

Traits of Good Writing — Grades 5-6

Teacher Created Resources

Author

Tracie Heskett, M. Ed.

Teacher Created Resources, Inc.
6421 Industry Way
Westminster, CA 92683
www.teachercreated.com
ISBN-1-4206-3593-X
©2006 Teacher Created Resources, Inc.
Made in U.S.A.

Table of Contents

Introduction

In the 1980s, teachers in the Northwest identified several traits, or characteristics, of effective student writing. These traits include Ideas and Content, Word Choice, Fluency, Voice, Organization, and Conventions and became known as "traits of good writing." Subsequently, educators added the trait of Presentation in keeping with state and national standards.

The purpose of this book is to provide teachers with practical, hands-on lesson plans to teach the traits of good writing in the classroom. Each section focuses on one trait, with lessons to teach the trait step-by-step to students. Lessons for each trait include lesson plans, reproducible pages for classroom use, and student samples, or documents, for use in the lessons.

Student samples in each section have a common theme or subject content area. Using themes will help give the lessons cohesiveness in the classroom presentation of each trait and may also assist teachers in incorporating the teaching of trait writing into their daily or weekly teaching schedules. That is, effective writing does not stand alone as something to be practiced in rote exercises but can be incorporated into all facets of student learning.

At the beginning of each section, you will find a poster that highlights the characteristics for the trait. These posters should be enlarged for display and referred to throughout the unit. Many lessons suggest making overhead transparencies or student copies of lesson material, specifically student samples. Teachers may also incorporate this material via scanner into PowerPoint or Smart Board™ presentations for classroom presentation. Students should keep their work in writing folders; many lessons use material students have completed in previous lessons.

Traits of Good Writing

- Ideas and Content

- Word Choice

- Fluency

- Voice

- Organization

- Conventions

- Presentation

Standards for Writing

The following standards are used by permission of McREL (Copyright 2000 MCREL, Mid-continent Research for Education and Learning. Telephone: 303-337-0990. Website: *http://www.mcrel.org*)

1. Demonstrates competence in the general skills and strategies of the writing process
   A. Prewriting: Uses prewriting strategies to plan written work (e.g., discusses ideas with peers, draws pictures to generate ideas, writes key thoughts and questions, rehearses ideas, records reactions and observations)
   B. Uses graphic organizers, story maps, and webs; groups related ideas; takes notes; brainstorms ideas
   C. Drafting and Revising: Uses strategies to draft and revise written work (e.g., rereads; rearranges words, sentences, and paragraphs to improve or clarify meaning; varies sentence type; adds descriptive words and details; deletes extraneous information; incorporates suggestions from peers and teachers; sharpens the focus)
   D. Elaborates on a central idea; uses paragraphs to develop separate ideas
   E. Editing and Publishing: Uses strategies to edit and publish written work (e.g., proofreads using a dictionary and other resources; edits for grammar, punctuation, capitalization, and spelling at a developmentally appropriate level; incorporates illustrations or photos; shares finished product)
   F. Evaluates own and others' writing (e.g., asks questions and makes comments about writing, helps classmates apply grammatical and mechanical conventions)
   G. Dictates or writes with a logical sequence of events (i.e., includes a beginning, middle, and ending)
   H. Dictates or writes detailed descriptions of familiar persons, places, objects, or experiences
   I. Writes in response to literature
   J. Writes in a variety of formats (e.g., picture books, letters, stories, poems, information pieces)
   K. Writes expressive composition (e.g., expresses ideas, reflections, and observations; uses an individual, authentic voice; uses relevant details; presents ideas that enable a reader to imagine the world of the event or experience)
   L. Writes autobiographical compositions (e.g., provides a context within which the incident occurs, uses simple narrative strategies, provides some insight into why this incident is memorable)
2. Develops awareness of the stylistic and rhetorical aspects of writing (i.e., sentence structure, rhythm)
   A. Uses general, frequently used words to convey basic ideas
   B. Uses descriptive language that clarifies and enhances ideas (e.g., describes familiar people, places, objects)
   C. Uses a variety of sentence structures
3. Uses grammatical and mechanical conventions in written compositions
4. Gathers and uses information for research purposes
   A. Generates questions about topics of personal interest
   B. Uses a variety of strategies to identify topics to investigate (e.g., brainstorms, lists questions, uses idea webs)
   C. Compiles information into oral reports
5. Demonstrates competence in speaking and listening as tools for learning
   A. Makes contributions in class and group discussions (e.g., recounts personal experiences, reports on personal knowledge about a topic, initiates conversations)
   B. Asks and responds to questions
   C. Reads compositions to the class
   D. Organizes ideas for oral presentation (e.g., includes content appropriate to the audience, uses notes or other memory aids, summarizes main points)
   E. Presents simple, prepared reports to the class

Standards Table

Lesson	Standard	Page Number
My Biome, My Home	1B, 2A, 4A, 4B	8
Exploring New Lands	1B, 1C, 2A, 2B, 4B, 4C, 5A	12
A World of Community	1B, 1D, 1F, 1K, 2B, 5A	15
Every Ecosystem Has a Story	1B, 1C, 1G, 1K, 2B, 5A	18
Welcome to My World	1A, 1B, 1C, 1D, 1F, 1J, 2, 4B, 5B	22
Word Pictures	1B, 1J, 2A, 2B, 4B	27
Expanding My Perspective	1A, 1H, 1K, 2A, 2B	30
Folktales Alive	1B, 1E, 1F, 1G, 1J, 2	32
The Sounds of Our Lives	1I, 1K, 2B	37
Describing My Culture	1B, 1C, 1D, 1F, 1H, 1L, 2B	40
Ocean Games	1K	45
It's Always Beautiful at the Beach	1B, 1C, 1D, 1F, 2C	48
Sea Swells	1B, 1C, 1E, 1J, 2B, 5C	51
"What If . . . ?"	1A, 1D, 1E, 1F, 1G, 1K, 5A, 5B	54
Putting It All Together	1B, 1C, 1E, 1G, 1J, 2, 5A, 5B, 5C	57
Getting to Know Jellanos	1B, 1F, 1J, 1K, 5A	62
Stepping Back in Time	1A, 1B, 1D, 1F, 1K, 2B, 4, 5	65
Calling My Reader	1B, 1F, 1J, 2B, 2C, 5A, 5B, 5C	68
Come Join the Quest	1B, 1C, 1E, 1F, 1J, 1K, 2	71
Bringing Writing to Life	1A, 1B, 1C, 1E, 1F, 1G, 1J, 3, 5A, 5C	75
Investigating Effective Writing	1A, 1B, 1C, 1G, 2, 4B	82
Step by Step	1F, 1G, 1J, 4C	86
Perfect Paragraphs	1C, 1D, 1F, 2C, 5A	89
Pathway to Rescue	1A, 1B, 1C, 1G, 1K, 2, 3	92
Why People Write	1B, 1C, 1D, 1E, 1J, 2, 3, 4B	95
The Mark of Excellence	1F, 3	102
Following the Laws	1F, 3	105
Let's All Agree	1F, 3	109
Strong Words Make Strong Writing	1F, 2, 3	114
It's All about Paragraphs	1D, 1F, 2, 3	116
Learning from Each Other	1F, 5B	119
A Display for All to See	1A, 1B, 2B, 4B, 4C	125
Preparing to Present	1A, 1B, 1D, 1J, 4C, 5B, 5D	129
Displaying My Information	2A, 2B, 4B, 4C, 5A, 5D	133
Final Stages of Planning	4C, 5A, 5B, 5D	136
My Presentation	1F, 5A, 5B, 5E	140

Ideas and Content

This trait lays the foundation for other aspects of effective student writing. Students need to learn to develop and organize their ideas and to present them clearly. Students should gather their ideas as well as research, seek new knowledge, and organize their information before they begin to write. Successful writers write about what they know, the subjects in which they have expertise, or specific knowledge and experience.

In practicing the characteristics of this trait, students identify topics about which they have prior knowledge, investigate and explore topics further by conducting additional research if needed, and learn to connect their writing to their own experiences.

Writing which is strong in content includes interesting, relevant, specific details and a development of the piece as a whole. Students will practice collecting ideas, writing about their own experiences, using examples and details, and writing complete pieces in which they can use insight and understanding to show readers what they know.

Ideas and Content

- use clear ideas

- use examples

- show, don't tell

- gather and organize ideas

- seek new knowledge, explore a topic

- connect writing to your own experience

- use interesting, relevant, specific details

- surprise the reader with what you know

- use insight and understanding

- develop your story, every piece adds to the whole

My Biome, My Home

Objective

Given instruction in organizing ideas, the students will create a web on a specific topic.

Materials

- white board, overhead projector, or chart paper and marker
- "Ideas and Content" poster (page 7), one copy for display
- "Organizing My Ideas" (page 10), one copy for display
- "My Home, the Desert" (page 11), one copy for display
- index cards, three per student
- children's dictionaries, one per student if possible
- white paper, 8 ½" x 11" (21.5 cm x 28 cm), one sheet per student
- picture books, cardstock for game cards (optional)

Preparation

Enlarge "Ideas and Content" poster (page 7), "My Home, the Desert" (page 11), and "Organizing My Ideas" (page 10) for display.

Opening

Introduce the "Ideas and Content" poster (page 7). Tell the students that this trait refers to the process of collecting and organizing ideas for clear, interesting, and effective writing.

Directions

1. Continue a class discussion on how writers gather ideas. Explain that writers begin with a topic, and they need to generate more specific ideas and thoughts about that topic before they begin to write.

2. Show the students "My Home, the Desert" (page 11). Explain how to create a web: write the topic in the center space. Write subtopics or ideas about the main topic on the outer lines. On the branches from the main lines, write details about each idea.

3. Display "Organizing My Ideas" (page 10). Demonstrate how the same principles applied to create a web may be used to complete other types of graphic organizers. That is, an author begins with a main topic, thinks of related ideas, and adds details and examples to expand on the topic.

4. Distribute three index cards to each student. Have the students find and write the definitions for *biome* and *ecosystem*. Have the students choose one biome (e.g., desert, forest, marsh, plains) to define as well.

5. Have the students refer to their definitions to create a web on a sheet of white paper about the biome they selected.

My Biome, My Home *(cont.)*

Closing

Have the students compare webs to see how their classmates organized their ideas. Ask the students to share what they have learned thus far about collecting ideas.

Extension

Have the students use a children's dictionary, picture books, and visual observation to collect interesting and unusual words. Students will use these words to create a picture book for a class of younger students. The book could be titled, *I Know These Words.* Or the students could create game cards for younger students to read as they play the game. Reading a card successfully would be worth one point; if a younger student contributes a word of his or her own, the student would receive two points for that turn.

Organizing My Ideas

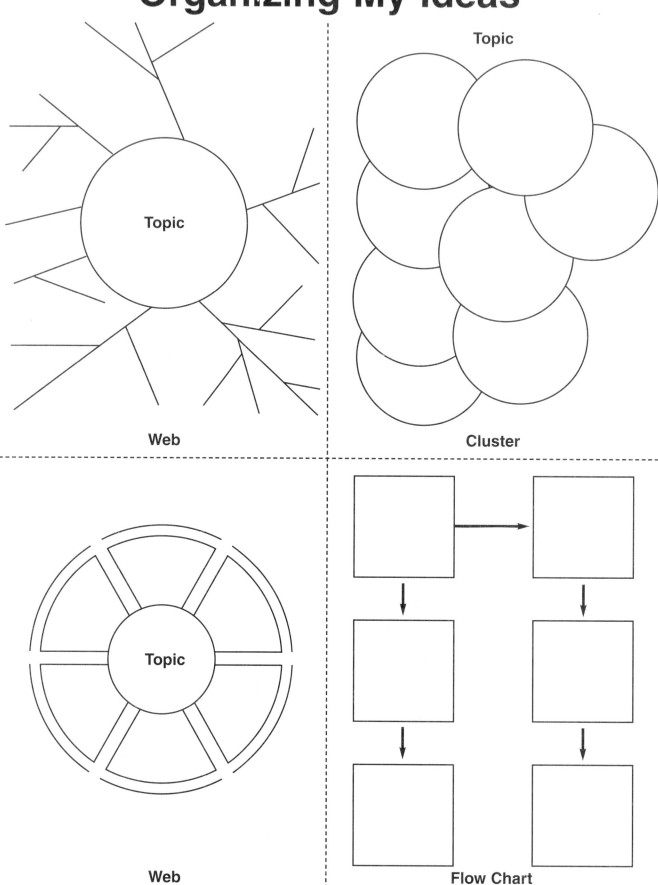

Topic

Web

Cluster

Topic

Web

Flow Chart

My Home, the Desert
by Charles C.

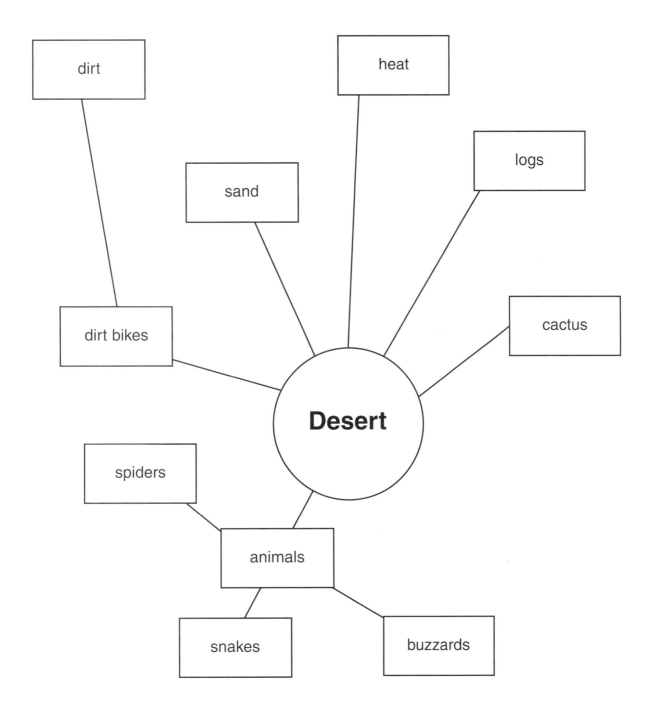

Exploring New Lands

Objective

Given instruction on research and taking notes, the students will investigate a topic and take notes to explore and compare similar topics.

Materials

- white board, overhead projector, or chart paper and marker
- guest speaker or video clip to describe a U.S. region
- "Deserts" (page 13), one copy for display
- classroom resources and pictures about biomes and geographic regions (e.g., magazines, pamphlets, brochures, maps, field guides)
- "Environments for Life" (page 14), one copy per student
- index cards, several per student
- award cutouts or ribbons (optional)

Preparation

Enlarge "Deserts" (page 13) for display.

Opening

Have a guest speaker who is an expert on a specific U.S. region talk to your class. Encourage the speaker to share details and examples, as well as his or her process of research and learning. Or, show a video clip that focuses on a specific U.S. region. If the speaker or video refers to one or more biomes that differ from your area, conduct a class discussion about the differences. Highlight any similarities as well.

Directions

1. Direct the students' attention to the "Ideas and Content" poster (page 7). Tell the class that sometimes in order to gather ideas about a specific topic, an author may need to explore the topic and gather additional information about the subject. Obtaining new knowledge requires research. Define *research* as "careful study and investigation to discover and explain new information." People who research study, read, and investigate other resources (e.g., interviewing people) to find out more about a topic.

2. Display for the students "Deserts" (page 13). Discuss with the class how the author took notes on what she read. She wrote short sentences, with just enough facts, to remind her of details. The author used her own words. The notes would fit on a single index card. Students could create one note card for each subtopic related to a main idea. Subtopics may be related to the lines or "spokes" on an idea web similar to "My Home, the Desert" (page 11).

Exploring New Lands *(cont.)*

Directions *(cont.)*

3. As a class, list several biomes, or geographical regions, on the white board. Have the students choose a biome about which they would like to conduct further research.

4. Distribute copies of "Environments for Life" (page 14). Have each student read and gather information about the subtopics indicated for his or her biome.

Closing

Ask the students to briefly present their biomes to the class or a small group. You might want to set up a "jigsaw" arrangement in which each group consists of students representing different biomes. Or, each group could be homogenous (i.e., representing the same biome) and the groups could later present their biomes to the rest of the class. As they share their information, the students should also state whether or not they would like to live in that environment and why.

Extension

Have the students write a paragraph about their biome using the information they gleaned from their research. Tell them to write a nonfiction piece as an "expert" on the subject. If you wish, give the students awards or ribbons for their paragraphs.

Deserts
by Taylor H.

Deserts are hot and have no lakes. Deserts have cacti and tumbleweeds. They also have no rain. The temperature is about 100°F.

Environments for Life

Biome: _____

Animals

Plants

Climate

A World of Community

Objective

Given experience taking notes and comparing them with others, the students will write a descriptive paragraph that includes details.

Materials

- white board, overhead projector, or chart paper and marker
- pictures of biomes from "Exploring New Lands" (page 12), at least one picture per student
- index cards, one per student
- "The Many Faces of Nature" (page 17), one copy for display (one copy per group, optional)
- "Mountains" (page 16)

Preparation

Enlarge "The Many Faces of Nature" (page 17) for display.

Opening

Show the students the "Ideas and Content" poster (page 7). Focus their attention on these characteristics: use interesting, relevant, specific details, and use clear ideas. Show the students one of the biome pictures from the previous lesson. Create a class web: ask the students to share details they notice in the picture. Tell the students that details may include specific features or aspects of the landscape or items they might include if they were writing trivia questions about the picture.

Directions

1. Continue a discussion on the concept of including details and clear ideas in writing. Explain that effective writing presents ideas in such a way that the reader can easily understand what is being said. You might compare this to clear water in a pond and murky water that has been stirred up. Clear water enables a person to see all the details of pond life. Authors should include relevant details that relate to the topic (e.g., in a paragraph about the forest, the reader would not find a sentence about the desert). Writing that has interesting details catches a reader's attention in such a way that he or she wants to know more about the topic. Interesting details may also add intrigue or excitement to the writing.

2. Give each student a picture of a biome and an index card. Ask the students to carefully observe the picture and imagine the scene, recalling any information they know about such a place. Have them write on the index card as many details about the picture as they can.

3. Have the students form homogenous groups based on biome (e.g., all students who had a desert picture would be in one group). Instruct the students to complete a web using their biome as the central topic. Group members should contribute details to add to the web.

A World of Community *(cont.)*

Closing

Change the student groups so that each group has one student representing each biome (e.g., each group would have a "forest" person, a "desert" person, and a "prairie" person). Show the class "The Many Faces of Nature" (page 17). Give each group a copy of page 17, if desired. Explain to the students that *World* is a central topic for the web. Group members will need to use one "spoke" of the web for each biome represented and cluster their specific details on that part of the web.

Extension

Read aloud "Mountains" (page 16). Conduct a brief class discussion about whether or not the author used interesting, relevant, and specific details. Regroup the students once again into homogenous groups by biome. Have the students write a group paragraph about their biome, including interesting, relevant, and specific details. One member of the group should read aloud the completed paragraph to the rest of the group. Students should ask themselves if the writing has clear ideas. When they hear the paragraph read aloud, can they easily understand the writing? Bind the group paragraphs into a class book entitled, *Biomes of Our World*. The book may be used in the classroom or donated to another class or the school library.

Mountains

by Caleb V.

I love mountains. They are fun to climb. You can play in many different places on a mountain, but make sure you don't get hurt by big boulders. Mountains can be scary to some people. Have you ever been on a mountain? People make many things out of rock like brick and other things. Rocks are made by lava.

The Many Faces of Nature

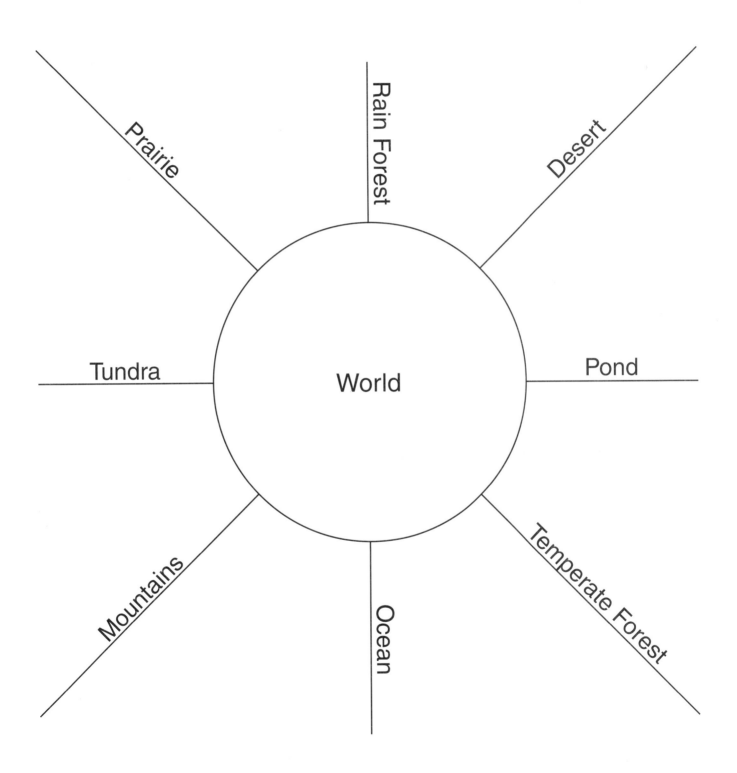

Every Ecosystem Has a Story

Objective

Given a graphic organizer and an introduction to developing a complete story, the students will fill out an idea page and use it to write a complete story.

Materials

- white board, overhead projector, or chart paper and marker
- "Finding Water" (page 20), one copy for display
- "Challenges in a Community" (page 21), one copy for display and one copy per student
- drawing paper and markers (optional)

Preparation

Enlarge "Finding Water" (page 20) and "Challenges in a Community" (page 21) for display.

Opening

Tell the class you will read a story aloud to them. Ask the students to listen carefully to determine whether or not each sentence and idea needs to be in the story. Everything the author included should add to the story; there should be no extra or unnecessary words or sentences. Ask the students to consider also how well the story shows action: did the author tell the reader what happened, or did they actually show action?

Directions

1. Read aloud "Finding Water" (page 20); then conduct a class discussion about developing a story and the practice of showing, rather than telling, action in a story. Tell the students that effective authors not only focus on their ideas, including those aspects of the Ideas and Content trait already considered, but they also pay careful attention to the overall content of their writing.

2. Show the students "Finding Water" (page 20). Read the story again, one sentence at a time. After each sentence, ask the students whether or not it contributes to the overall story. If it does not, draw a line through the sentence.

3. Display "Challenges in a Community" (page 21). Ask the students to contribute ideas as you complete the graphic organizer together using "Finding Water" (page 20) as a sample. Explain that the *problem* in a story refers to the "conflict or struggle the main character faces." The character must take action to solve the problem or resolve the conflict; the students should list specific things the character does in the story. The *solution* is "how the character solves the problem, resolves the conflict, or ends the struggle."

Every Ecosystem Has a Story *(cont.)*

Directions *(cont.)*

4. Distribute copies of "Challenges in a Community" (page 21). Tell the students their story will need to have one or more characters, a problem or conflict, action to solve the problem, and a solution. Their story will take place in one specific biome and the conflict in the story will relate to that ecosystem (e.g., the ecosystem breaks down in some way).

Closing

Have the students use page 21 to write a complete story about that particular biome and ecosystem. Evaluate student writing based on use of details, clear ideas, how well the story shows action, and overall development of the story.

Extension

Divide the class into small groups. Distribute drawing paper and markers to the students. Assign each student a biome; each student in a group will have a different biome from other members of the group. Have the students take turns illustrating one or two features of their biome without speaking. Other members in the group should try to guess which biome is represented in the illustration. Students will take turns illustrating and guessing; each time it is their turn, they will add one or two more features to the drawing in such a way that each piece adds to the whole picture of a biome. You may wish to display completed pictures on a bulletin board featuring biomes and ecosystems.

Finding Water

by Kenneth M.

Soggy the squirrel yawned. He had just settled down for his long winter nap. Soggy lived in the Columbia River Gorge near Portland, Oregon, which explained his name. As he lay in his well-made bed, high up in a Douglas fir tree, he grew thirsty. Sighing, he got up and wandered to the lake for the last drink until spring. As he approached the lake, however, it was dry! It had dried up overnight! Soggy sat down and did some serious thinking. He would be all right through the winter; he could sleep through it. His friends would need to be warned. They would have to move to another forest area, one with some water. Unfortunately, only Soggy knew where that area was, and his body had already started to shut down. This would call for quick action, fast feet, and good thinking. He didn't have a second to lose.

Soggy's first task was to locate Buzz, the beaver. He would know about the water situation and be eager to find an alternate source. Buzz's dam was indeed dry and Buzz was in a bad temper. He had worked all summer and stored enough food for his whole family. Due to no water, the dam had collapsed and Buzz's family had barely gotten out alive. Soggy made it to Buzz's just in time to stop them from trying to rebuild. Soggy told Buzz and his family that humans had drained the lake and taken the water. Luckily, he knew where to find more water, but poor Soggy was too tired to tell everyone. Buzz agreed to carry Soggy, and Buzz's family split up. Together they would find Soggy's friends and tell them about the secret new lake. Morning and afternoon passed. Soggy's body was almost asleep.

The two friends still had to find two more families. Hooty the owl and Trace the snake both had to be found, and quickly. Just as night began to darken the December sky, a noise came from a bush. It was Trace! Soggy was very tired by now. But night was approaching, and if Hooty was not found . . . . Soggy forced himself wide awake, and told Buzz's family to go ahead to the new lake. He would find Hooty and his family.

Darkness approached swiftly. Soggy had been up half the trees and had seen no sign of Hooty. Desperate, Soggy took to jumping trees to save time, calling out for Hooty. By now, Soggy had no strength left. With a third of the trees left unsearched, Soggy fell from a high branch. There, his body gave up, and halfway down, he fell asleep. He awoke to a pair of fluffy wings. Hooty! Hooty had caught Soggy! Soggy quickly told Hooty about the lake. Hooty thanked him and flew him to a tree next to the new lake. He promised to tell his family about the new lake. Glad that all his friends were safe, Soggy fell asleep, cozy and safe.

Challenges in a Community

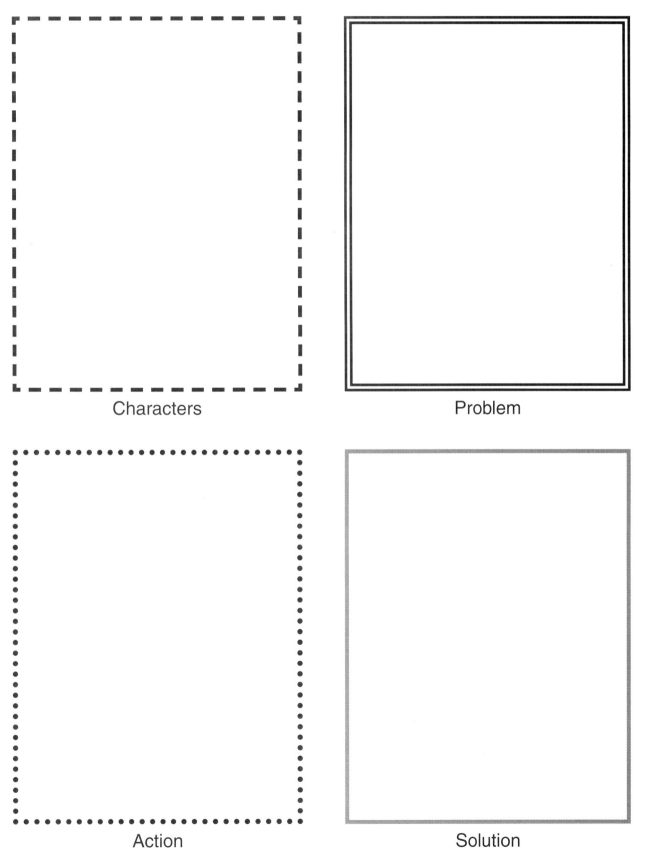

Characters

Problem

Action

Solution

Welcome to My World

Objective

Given a review of the characteristics of the Ideas and Content trait, the students will use previous research to write a nonfiction article.

Materials

- "The Rain Forest" (page 23), one copy per student

- colored pencils, six different colors per student

- student work from previous lessons

- classroom resources about biomes and ecosystems (e.g., books, magazines, pamphlets) from previous lessons

- "Learning about Communities" (page 24), one copy per student

Opening

Review the "Ideas and Content" poster (page 7). Explain that when authors gather ideas, research, seek new knowledge, and use clear ideas and specific examples, they can surprise the reader with what they know. As authors incorporate aspects of the Ideas and Content trait, they will write with insight and understanding, which will make their writing more effective and interesting to the reader.

Directions

1. Tell the students that writers often use their research, knowledge, and expertise about a specific topic to write nonfiction articles to share information with others. Explain that a nonfiction article differs from a story in that it does not have fictional characters but is based on fact. Nonfiction writing often follows a format that includes who, what, where, when, why, and how.

2. Distribute copies of "The Rain Forest" (page 23). Ask the students to identify specific parts of the nonfiction article: who, what, where, when, why, and how. Students should use a different colored pencil to mark each element: blue for *who*, red for *what*, orange for *where*, green for *when*, yellow for *why*, and purple for *how*.

3. At the bottom of page 23, have the students write two or three sentences telling how the author surprised the reader with what he knew, and how the author used insight and understanding in the writing.

4. Ensure that the students have copies of previous work completed during the study of the Ideas and Content trait, specifically research notes about biomes. Distribute copies of "Learning about Communities" (page 24). Have the students use their notes to complete the graphic organizer as they plan to write a nonfiction article about their biome.

Welcome to My World *(cont.)*

Closing

Ask the students to write two facts on the back of "Learning about Communities" (page 24) to include in their nonfiction article that will surprise their reader with what they know. Have them also write one sentence telling how they will use their insight and understanding to write about their biome. Direct the students to use the completed idea page to write a nonfiction article about the biome.

Extension

Ask the students to write interview questions that they can ask a classmate to learn about his or her biome. Have the students use their questions to interview another student about his or her biome. Students may refer to their nonfiction articles or research notes to answer interview questions.

The Rain Forest

by Justin V.

There is a lot of information about the rain forest. There are a lot of rain forests in danger. The rain forests are home to over half a million species.

One-quarter of the medicines that we use today are derived from plants. Exotic orchids, sneaky jaguars, big armadillos, colorful songbirds, noisy monkeys, and elusive snakes are but some of the creatures that inhabit tropical rain forests. Nearly half of Earth's original forest cover has already been lost, and each year more than 30 million tropical rain forest acres are destroyed.

Learning about Communities

Where

My biome is: _____

Who

These people live in this place: _____

_____

You would find these animals in this biome: _____

_____

_____

What

These are some problems or issues in this ecosystem: _____

_____

This is something that has happened in this biome: _____

_____

_____

When

This is when these things have happened: _____

_____

_____

Why

This is why my biome has these problems: _____

_____

_____

How

This is how the problems can be solved: _____

_____

_____

scorching   precious   sluggish   awful   joyous   clumsy   noisy

Word Choice

Paying attention to Word Choice enables students to write effectively, in such a way that the reader will understand and want to read their writing. Elements of the Word Choice trait include using strong, visual imagery and descriptive writing. Writers learn to use accurate and precise words to say exactly what they want to communicate. Specific words convey distinct meanings. Students should use action words to give their writing energy, as well as descriptive nouns and adjectives. Using effective word choice implies a familiarity with the language, as students learn to use parts of speech and subject-verb agreement properly. An effective writer listens to how words sound, using words that sound natural and add to the meaning of the writing.

As students learn about the Word Choice trait, they will practice writing descriptive pieces, writing a story with action verbs, and writing dialogue. Students will also participate in a listening activity, as well as write for a specific purpose, expanding their perspective by observing and then writing.

stormy   dizzy   horrible   jittery   itchy   honest

gigantic   teeny   big   miniscule   mammoth

delicious   zany   beautiful   scrawny

Word Choice

- write with *descriptive words*

- use strong visual imagery

- use accurate and precise words to convey a specific meaning

- understand that action verbs give writing energy

- be familiar with language

- use words that sound natural

- listen to how words sound, adding to the meaning of the writing

Word Pictures

Objective

Given classroom resources and a review of basic parts of speech, the students will gather words to create a word collage.

Materials

- white board, overhead projector, or chart paper and marker
- "Word Choice" poster (page 26), one copy for display
- magazine picture or photograph of an object, event, place, or scene
- "Word Walk" (page 29), one copy per student
- student dictionaries and thesauruses
- "My Word Picture" (page 28), one copy for display
- "Culture: A Way of Life" (page 29), one copy per student
- construction paper, 9" x 12" (23 cm x 30 cm), one sheet per student
- markers
- magazines or newspapers (optional)

Preparation

Enlarge the "Word Choice" poster (page 26) and "My Word Picture" (page 28) for display. Enlarge "Word Walk" and "Culture: A Way of Life" (page 29) to 8 ½" x 11" (21.5 cm x 28 cm) and photocopy.

Opening

Show the class the picture or photograph of an object, event, place, or scene. Have the students describe the picture using one word at a time. Ask the students what types of words they used to describe the picture (adjectives). Review definitions and examples of nouns, verbs, and adverbs. You may need to remind the students that adjectives usually modify nouns, and adverbs modify verbs. Explain that knowing about different types of words helps writers choose the most appropriate words to make their writing as strong and effective as possible.

Directions

1. Show the "Word Choice" poster (page 26) to the students. Discuss with the students the first and third aspects of the Word Choice trait: effective writing contains descriptive words and accurate and precise words intended to convey a specific meaning. That is, authors choose their words carefully to say exactly what they want to communicate.

2. Distribute copies of "Word Walk" (page 29). Explain that the students will go on a scavenger hunt for words. They may gather words from dictionaries, thesauruses or classroom books. Encourage the students to collect as many interesting words as possible. They should write each word in the appropriate column of page 29, indicating noun, verb, adjective, or adverb.

Word Pictures *(cont.)*

Directions *(cont.)*

3. Display "My Word Picture" (page 28). Ask the students to read the words on the collage and try to guess which word the author chose for a topic word.

4. Distribute copies of "Culture: A Way of Life" (page 29). Tell the students that *culture* refers to "a way of life." Culture may include ideas, customs, traditions, skills, and the arts (music, painting, books) of a group of people. Ask the students to choose a word related to the word *culture* for their beginning word. They should write the beginning word on the top "stem" of the cluster. Have them write words related to or defining their word in the other circles in the cluster.

Closing

Give each student a sheet of construction paper. Tell the students they will make a word collage, or word picture, about the word they chose. (They should not write the actual word on the page.) They may use markers or letters cut from magazines or newspapers to write words from their graphic organizer on the collage page. Have the students display their collages. Students may try to guess the words depicted on their classmates' collages.

Extension

Briefly define for the students the concept of *simile* and *metaphor*. Post the magazine pictures or photographs of an object, event, place, or scene for student viewing. Ask a volunteer to choose one picture and identify that picture for the class. Have the students think of ways the picture may be compared to everyday items. Explain that similes and metaphors provide ways for authors to write descriptions. Model a simile or metaphor for the class using the selected picture. Ask the students to select one or more pictures about which to write their own metaphors or similes.

My Word Picture
by Charles C.

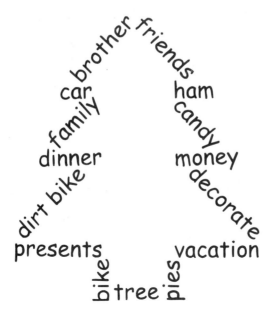

Word Walk

Nouns	Verbs	Adjectives	Adverbs

Culture: A Way of Life

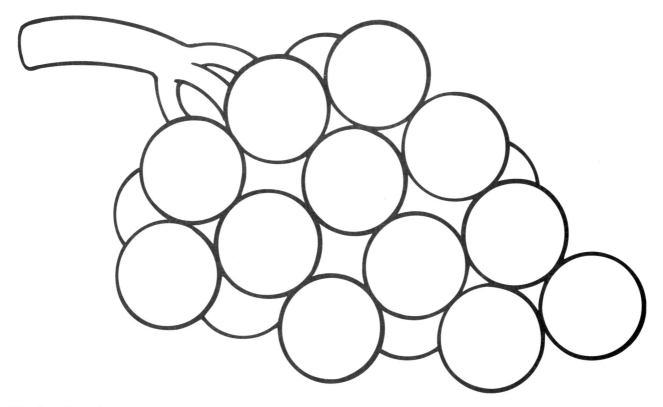

Expanding My Perspective

Objective

Given an introduction to the characteristics of the Word Choice trait, the students will use words to create a graphic design.

Materials

- white board, overhead projector, or chart paper and marker
- "My Favorite Place" (page 31)
- white paper, 8 ½" x 11" (21.5 cm x 28 cm), one sheet per student
- colored pencils or crayons
- assortment of common classroom items
- white construction paper and markers (optional)
- "My Word Picture" (page 28) (optional)
- white construction paper, 9" x 12" (23 cm x 30 cm), one sheet per student (optional)

Opening

Show the students the "Word Choice" poster (page 26). Introduce the concept: writers choose words carefully to convey a specific visual picture or meaning. Descriptive words create visual imagery; words help readers expand their perspective and form a mental picture. Define *imagery* as "mental pictures formed in part by memory or imagination;" a mental picture is an "image seen in the mind" that is not actually present in the person's vision, or what he or she sees at that moment.

Directions

1. Give each student a sheet of white paper. Tell the class you will read aloud a descriptive paragraph. Have the students listen carefully and draw a picture of the place they envision in their mind. Students may use colored pencils or crayons to draw their pictures.

2. Read aloud "My Favorite Place" (page 31); then ask students to offer words they heard in the story that helped them visualize the place as they drew their pictures. List these descriptive words on the white board. Have students add other words to the list that could have helped them form a better mental picture or image.

3. Review the concepts of *metaphor* and *simile:* authors use descriptive words to compare two different things. A simile includes the words *like* or *as* (e.g., the sky was as blue as a robin's egg).

4. Display the assorted items. Have the students work independently or with a partner to write similes and metaphors to compare the items. You may wish to generate a class word bank of descriptive words on the white board before students begin this activity.

Expanding My Perspective *(cont.)*

Closing

Have the students use descriptive words, as well as what they have learned about similes and metaphors, to write a description of their favorite place. They will trade papers with a partner and draw a picture of the place their partner described. Partners will then give feedback on the accuracy of the drawings and which words especially helped them draw the picture.

Extension

Have the students consider their culture, or way of life. Culture may include ideas, customs, traditions, skills, and the arts (music, painting, books) of a group of people. Distribute sheets of white construction paper. Have the students use markers to write words to describe their culture. They should arrange the words as "word art" or a graphic design. Refer to "My Word Picture" (page 28) from the previous lesson to help explain this concept.

My Favorite Place

by Cody H.

My place is under a bridge. It is kind of cold. You hear skateboards and a lot of yelling. My place is the Burnside Skatepark. You don't smell or taste much, but you do hear a lot of things. You see ramps; you see bowls. Oh, I almost forgot, you see quarter pipes. There are people jumping off the ramps and quarter pipes and there are people grinding in the bowls. This is my favorite place.

Folktales Alive

Objective

Given a review of the parts of speech and synonyms, the students will create a story using action verbs.

Materials

- American folktale picture books (e.g., *Johnny Appleseed, Paul Bunyan, Pecos Bill, Davy Crockett*), one per group
- sticky notes, at least one per student
- student dictionaries and thesauruses
- "People, Places, Actions" (page 36), one copy per student
- "Johnny Appleseed" (page 34)
- sample strip book (page 33), (optional)
- strip book pattern (page 35), two copies per student and two copies for sample (optional)
- colored construction paper, 9" x 12" (23 cm x 30 cm), one sheet per student and one sheet for sample (optional)
- stapler (optional)
- art supplies to decorate book covers (optional)

Preparation

To complete the sample strip book, make two copies of page 35 and cut on the heavy, solid boarder line. Fold the papers lengthwise along the middle solid line. Write an adjective in the first row, a noun in the second row, a verb in the third row, and an adverb in the fourth row. (See sample strip book pages on page 33 for corresponding words.) Cut along the dotted lines to create strips (do not cut all the way to the fold). Staple the four pages between a folded sheet of construction paper.

Opening

Review again the parts of speech: noun, verb, adjective, and adverb. Have the students define *action verb*. Ask the students why using action verbs would give writing energy and make it more interesting to the reader. Discuss the concept of *synonyms* and ask the students to give examples. Have the students express why an author might want to use a synonym and be familiar with synonyms as he or she writes.

Directions

1. Divide the class into small groups. Distribute a folktale picture book to each group. Give each student at least one sticky note. As the students read the picture book, they should write words of interest, especially action verbs, on the note.
2. Have the students use a thesaurus to find synonyms for the action verbs and other words of interest from the story.
3. Distribute copies of "People, Places, Actions" (page 36). Have the students work independently to complete the graphic organizer about the story they just read.

Folktales Alive *(cont.)*

Directions *(cont.)*

4. Read aloud "Johnny Appleseed" (page 34). Ask the students if they recognize the folktale. How did they know which original story the author had in mind?

5. Have the students identify action verbs and synonyms in the story. Discuss how the author changed some elements in the story yet kept the flavor of the original story. Ask the students to use their synonym notes and "People, Places, Action" (page 36) to rewrite the folktale. They may change the characters or setting, but the flavor of the tale should remain the same.

Closing

Ask the students to share their folktales with the class. Have the students give one another feedback on how effectively they used action verbs, synonyms, and other descriptive words.

Extension

Show the students the sample strip book and explain how it was made (see Preparation, page 32). Demonstrate how the strips can be moved to create different stories.

Students may use their notes and rewritten folktales to create strip books for a younger class. Give each student a sheet of colored construction paper and two copies of page 35. Have the students write an adjective in the first space of a page and a noun in the second space. Tell the students an adverb simply tells how or when something happened. Instruct the students to write a verb in the third space and an adverb in the fourth space. Tell the students an adverb simply tells how or when something happened. Students should place their story-strip pages inside a sheet of folded construction paper. Staple the booklets, if possible. Have the students decorate the cover of their booklet.

Sample Strip Book Pages

Seven	Blue
men	"Babe"
chopped	pulled
quickly.	vigorously.

Johnny Appleseed

by Susan R.

One day a man came walking through the meadow. He carried a burlap sack across his shoulders and wore pants torn almost to his knee. I wondered where he came from and why he was here.

I said, "Howdy," and he waved back.

The strange man approached and told me his name was Johnny Appleseed.

"That's a different name," I said. "What are you doing in this part of the country?"

"I'm planting apple trees," he replied, patting his sack. "May I plant a few on your land?"

"Certainly," I said. I invited him to stay and have supper with us. After we ate, he gathered the children around and told stories of where he had been and where he planned to go.

The next morning he prepared to continue his journey across America planting apple seeds. We wished him well as he set out. If you eat an apple today, you can thank Johnny Appleseed.

Strip Book Pattern

People, Places, Actions

Places

People

Actions

The Sounds of Our Lives

Objective

Given a listening activity, the students will take notes and add interpretation to clarify meaning.

Materials

- "Fourth of July" (page 38)
- "I Hear the Words" (page 39), one copy per student
- poster board or chart paper and marker (optional)
- puppets or materials to make puppets (e.g., socks or small paper bags, markers, bits of fabric or felt, yarn) (optional)

Preparation

If students are making their own puppets, have them draw faces on socks or small paper bags and add details using other craft materials.

Opening

Tell the class that effective writing includes words that sound natural; how words sound also adds to the meaning. Some words have specific sounds that help the reader know what the word means.

Directions

1. Tell the students you will read them a paragraph. As you read, they will write words that especially add to the meaning of the writing. These words might be words that have definite sounds relating to the meaning of the word (e.g., *buzz*).

2. Distribute copies of "I Hear the Words" (page 39). Read aloud "Fourth of July" (page 38). Have the students take notes on page 39 as you read. After you read the sample, you may need to suggest one or two words to help students think about words in this way. Read "Fourth of July" (page 38) again, if necessary, to give students another opportunity to write words.

3. Discuss with the students the concept of *interpretation*: an author should use words that help the reader understand the meaning of the writing. Draw the students' attention to #4 on "I Hear the Words" (page 39). Have the students write the main idea the author wanted to express.

Closing

Discuss the students' responses to "Fourth of July" (page 38). Ask the students what they have learned about Word Choice thus far. How can authors select effective words? You might want to list the students' suggestions and create a poster for display to help your students in their writing.

The Sounds of Our Life *(cont.)*

Extension

Have the students work in small groups to create a puppet skit about word choice. Students should take notes as they work to use as a script when presenting to the class. Puppet skits might feature words that sound natural compared to words that try to impress or exaggerate, a discussion on words that have specific sounds that add to meaning, or characters that know and have familiarity with the language and characters that do not. Have the groups share their puppet skits with the class.

Fourth of July

by Kelly C.

Every year we celebrate the Fourth of July. Once our family went to the park to watch a fireworks show. We got there before it got dark, and my sister and I splashed in the creek. We started to sing, but then we heard a loud bang! We looked around to see if anyone had any fireworks, but it was just my brother. He put air in an empty bag and popped it. It really surprised us!

We all went back to our picnic table to have dinner. I could hear the hot dogs sizzle as they roasted on the grill. I looked forward to the crunchy carrot sticks and dip, too.

Soon it got dark and we waited for the fireworks to start. Suddenly, there was a hush over the crowd, and we saw the first firework in the air. Bang! It almost hurt my ears. The bang was so loud! I heard the next firework pop and I said, "Wow!" when I saw all the vibrant colors. We had a great time watching all the fireworks during the Fourth of July celebration.

I Hear the Words

Read the questions and write your answers on the lines below.

1. List the author's words that have specific sounds (for example, *buzz*).

_____

_____

_____

2. Which words added to the meaning of the writing?

_____

_____

_____

3. Which words helped you understand what the author was trying to say?

_____

_____

_____

4. What is the main idea the author wanted to express?

_____

_____

_____

Describing My Culture

Objective

Given a review of the characteristics of the Word Choice trait, the students will write a paper using descriptive language.

Materials

- student items (see Preparation)
- "America" (page 41)
- "Our Culture" (page 42), one copy per student
- colored pencils, one per student
- colored construction paper, 9" x 12" (23 cm x 30 cm), one sheet per student (optional)
- white paper, 8½" x 11" (21.5 cm x 28 cm), several sheets per student (optional)
- markers, stickers, decorative scissors, other craft items (optional)

Preparation

Have the students bring one small item from home that represents their culture, or way of life.

Opening

Remind the students of the definition of *culture* as "a way of life;" culture may include ideas, customs, traditions, skills, and the arts (music, painting, books) of a group of people. Have as many students as time allows share the items they brought from home. Each student should explain how the item represents his or her way of life.

Directions

1. Review with the students the "Word Choice" poster (page 26). Point out that effective writing includes descriptive words that accurately portray what the author intends to say.

2. Tell the students they will use descriptive language to write a paper about their culture. They may focus specifically on their family, school, or community.

3. Read aloud "America" (page 41). Ask the students to identify ways in which the writing exhibits qualities of the Word Choice trait. You might want to refer to the "Word Choice Poster" (page 26) and ask students about each characteristic.

4. Distribute copies of "Our Culture" (page 42). Have the students use this as an idea page to gather and organize their ideas about the topic. Encourage the students to consider the aspects of Word Choice as they choose words to write on the web. They should also use these descriptive words when they write their paper.

5. Have the students use page 42 to write a paper. Their papers should include a paragraph for each main idea they want to express; they should have at least three paragraphs. You may wish to modify the length requirement, depending on your class.

Describing My Culture *(cont.)*

Closing

Have the students swap papers with a partner. You might want to have the students hide their names so that papers are exchanged anonymously. Ask the students to use a colored pencil to circle accurate, precise, descriptive words that add to visual imagery, convey a specific meaning, or sound natural.

Extension

Have the students write simple sentences to describe the general culture of the community. They should illustrate their sentences to make a picture book for younger students. Each student may make their own picture book containing up to 10 pages. Bind the books and have the students present them to a younger class.

America
by Lucas S.

I'm here to tell you about America. We have good food like pizza, spaghetti, and macaroni and cheese. My favorite is pizza. We have Christmas and Hanukkah here. During the holidays, you get to see your family. You get presents. It is fun!

Our Culture

Games

_____

_____

_____

_____

_____

Food

_____

_____

_____

_____

House

_____

_____

_____

_____

_____

Clothes

_____

_____

_____

_____

Traditions

_____

_____

_____

_____

School

_____

_____

_____

_____

Fluency

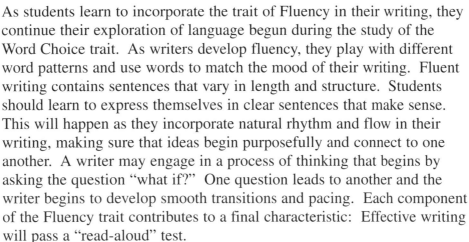

As students learn to incorporate the trait of Fluency in their writing, they continue their exploration of language begun during the study of the Word Choice trait. As writers develop fluency, they play with different word patterns and use words to match the mood of their writing. Fluent writing contains sentences that vary in length and structure. Students should learn to express themselves in clear sentences that make sense. This will happen as they incorporate natural rhythm and flow in their writing, making sure that ideas begin purposefully and connect to one another. A writer may engage in a process of thinking that begins by asking the question "what if?" One question leads to another and the writer begins to develop smooth transitions and pacing. Each component of the Fluency trait contributes to a final characteristic: Effective writing will pass a "read-aloud" test.

As students learn about the Fluency trait, they will practice writing in a variety of formats. They will gather words to create word patterns and to match specific moods. One lesson will introduce poetry as a further way to explore language. Students will also evaluate one another, reviewing traits studied thus far as they participate in read aloud activities.

Fluency

- play with language and words

- use different word patterns

- use appropiate words to match the mood of the piece

- vary sentence length and structure

- write clear sentences that make sense

- write with natural rhythm and flow

- use the process of thinking, "What if?"

- make sure ideas begin purposefully and connect to one another

- try the "read-aloud" test

Ocean Games

Objective

Given a script, the students will act out words to match a mood and practice playing with words and creating patterns by participating in a game.

Materials

- white board, overhead projector, or chart paper and marker
- "Fluency" poster (page 44), one copy for display
- "Calm Seas, Stormy Seas" (page 46), one copy for every four groups
- "Words to Match My Mood" (page 47), one copy per group (optional)
- cardstock (optional)
- index cards, two or three per student (optional)
- ocean-related costumes (optional)

Preparation

Enlarge the "Fluency" poster (page 44) for display. Make one copy of "Calm Seas, Stormy Seas" (page 46). Cut apart sections so that each group will have one. You may wish to have multiple copies of each section for group members. Enlarge and photocopy "Words to Match My Mood" (page 47) onto cardstock. Only cut apart the Descriptive Words game cards.

Opening

Introduce the "Fluency" poster (page 44). Tell the students that the qualities of Fluency are closely related to the Word Choice trait; writers choose and arrange words in such a way that the words match the mood of the writing. The writing makes sense, has natural rhythm, and flows smoothly.

Directions

1. Further explain the concept of word patterns by telling the class that a *pattern* is a design arranged for artistic effect. Writers also arrange words to achieve a particular effect. Longer words may make the writing flow more smoothly; words that rhyme may add some rhythm to the piece. Writers should not be afraid to play with words, rearranging them and trying different words until they have just the right combination to say exactly what they want. Playing and experimenting with words also helps writers become more familiar with the language.

2. Tell the students that they will work in a small group to read and act out a skit. Students will not have any lines to read or say; their skit will be a charade.

3. Divide the students into small groups and distribute a copy of one section of "Calm Seas, Stormy Seas" (page 46) to each group. Allow time for the students to read, act out, and practice their skit. If ocean costumes are available, the students may wear them while presenting their skit to the class.

Ocean Games *(cont.)*

Directions *(cont.)*

4. Have each group present their skit; classmates may guess which mood each skit portrays.

Closing

Have the students write a reflective paragraph or journal entry about their experiences playing with words. Did they learn any new words that they can use again in their writing? What did they learn about word patterns that will help them in their writing?

Extension

Have the students play a game using the "Words to Match My Mood" game cards (page 47). Divide the students into small groups. Each group will need one copy of both sets of game cards. Students will also add their own words to the game by writing words on half-sized index cards. To play the game, place all cards from the Descriptive Words deck facedown in a pile. Place the Mood Word grid faceup. Each student will take turns drawing four cards from the Descriptive Words deck. He or she will arrange the cards in a phrase to describe the ocean, adding his or her own words as necessary. The student will then choose an appropriate Mood Word to match the phrase. Have the student write the phrase and Mood Word on a sheet of paper for evaluation, if desired. At the end of a turn, the student will place the game cards at the bottom of the deck. When all the cards in the deck have been used, the deck should be shuffled to continue play.

Calm Seas, Stormy Seas

A. Your sea is calm with light waves and surf. The sky has a few clouds, perhaps a little fog or mist. There is no wind. The sand is damp.
B. The sun is shining, but the wind is blowing. The sun glitters off the waves, and a few waves have white caps. Dry sand blows around.
C. You have a very stormy sea. The wind blows the rain almost sideways. Huge waves pound and crash on the shore. The sky is almost black with many heavy clouds. The sand is wet.
D. You have a gray sea and a gray sky. There is a steady rain but no wind. Everything is the same color. The sand is damp or wet. The waves are mostly flat, with the surf beaten down by the rain.

Words to Match My Mood

Descriptive Words

fair	marine	saltwater	gray	threatening
calm	serene	bright	crashing	overcast
foul	turbulent	stormy	rough	dark
clear	churning	pounding	ominous	smooth

Mood Words

peaceful	excited	afraid
sad	frustrated	uncertain
bored	confident	joyful

It's Always Beautiful
at the Beach

Objective

Given instruction and sample sentences, the students will identify various sentence structures and clear writing and will write sentences exhibiting qualities of the Fluency trait.

Materials

- white board, overhead projector, or chart paper and marker
- "Dolphins" (page 49), one copy per student
- "Playing in the Waves" (page 50), one copy per student
- small stickers (three different colors), three or four per student (optional)

Opening

Tell the students that one way in which authors can create a particular mood, emotion, or attitude in their writing is to use a variety of sentence lengths and structures. Not all sentences begin the same or are the same length. Sometimes writers will use a simple sentence to make a point, and other times they will use a complex sentence to make the writing more interesting. Ask the students what they think the phrase, "write clear sentences" means. Explain that *clear* means "precise or easy to understand;" the reader has no doubt as to what the sentence means, nothing hinders the reader's understanding, and the sentence makes sense.

Directions

1. Review with the class various types of sentences: statements, questions, and exclamations. Demonstrate simple, compound, and complex sentences on the white board. Show the students how words may be arranged differently within a sentence (i.e., a sentence that begins with subject-verb or a sentence that begins with a prepositional phrase and has the subject-verb later in the sentence).

2. Distribute copies of "Dolphins" (page 49). Tell the students they will read the sample sentences. If the students will use stickers, explain what each color represents. If you do not plan to use stickers, draw for the students three or four symbols (e.g., circle, star, triangle, square) they may use to show each concept. They will place a sticker or draw a symbol by each sentence to show if the sentence is clear and easy to understand, as well as using appropriate stickers or symbols to show different types and structures of sentences.

3. Review together the students' responses. Then ask the students to review types of sentences and various sentence structures. Write the students' responses on the white board.

It's Always Beautiful at the Beach *(cont.)*

Closing

Distribute copies of "Playing in the Waves" (page 50). Have the students write sentences about the ocean on this page. Encourage the students to ensure their sentences make sense and are easy for the reader to understand.

Extension

Have the students rewrite their sentences on "Playing in the Waves" (page 50) to form a complete paragraph(s) about the ocean. Encourage the students to practice what they have learned previously about Word Choice and expand on their thoughts from page 50.

Dolphins

by Kaylee B.

Most dolphins are baby blue.

I have never seen one a different color.

They're curved and very beautiful.

Dolphins are about the smartest animals I know.

They live to be about 20 years old.

They swim in herds.

Unlike fish, dolphins live mainly at the top of the sea because they have to come up to get air.

Dolphins have blow holes to breathe through and also a tail and a flipper.

Playing in the Waves

1. The (A, An) _____ _____.
    (circle one)   noun   verb

2. (It, They) _____ _____.
    (circle one)   verb   adverb

3. _____ (has, have) _____
            noun   (circle one)   adjective

    _____.
            noun

4. _____ (it, they) _____,
            adverb   (circle one)   verb

    _____ _____.
            noun   verb

5. _____ _____
            noun   verb

    _____ the (a, an) _____
          preposition   (circle one)   noun

    _____ the (a, an) _____,
          preposition   (circle one)   noun

    and (it, they) _____ _____.
    (circle one)   verb   prepositional phrase

Sea Swells

Objective

Given further instruction in characteristics of Fluency and a lesson on writing poetry, the students will practice poetic forms and write poetry about the ocean.

Materials

- published poetry about the ocean
- "Sea" (page 52)
- "Rhythm Has Many Forms" (page 53), one copy per student
- colored construction paper, 9" x 12" (23 cm x 30 cm), one sheet per student (optional)
- stickers, construction-paper scraps, decorative scissors, glue, markers, photographs (optional)

Opening

Ask the students to describe poetry. How is poetry different from narrative writing? Ask the students to express what they like about poetry. Read aloud published poems about the ocean.

Directions

1. Ask the students what they observed about the poetry you read. How did the authors use words, phrases, and sentences? What types of rhythm or rhyme did they hear in the poems? What moods did the poetry express?

2. Read aloud "Sea" (page 52). Discuss how the poem shows natural rhythm or flow.

3. Continue a discussion about writing poetry. Point out that poetry often rhymes but not always. Poems may not have complete sentences in narrative form; instead they may be composed of word phrases. Poetry often expresses experiences or emotion and uses descriptive words with strong, visual imagery. Tell the students that poetry has rhythm even if it does not rhyme; explain that most song lyrics are written as poetry. Poets often arrange words in patterns. A poet may play with the language, putting words in an order the reader may not expect. Or the poet might write a silly poem.

4. Distribute copies of "Rhythm Has Many Forms" (page 53). Review each type of poetic form with the class. *Haiku* is a form of Japanese poetry, which in English has three unrhymed lines of five, seven, and five syllables each. The topic of a haiku is usually about nature. *Couplets* are two rhymed lines with stressed and unstressed syllables. A *cinquain* has five lines (see page 53). Or a *free verse* poem may not follow any of these forms directly as in "Sea" (page 52).

5. Have the students use "Rhythm Has Many Forms" (page 53) to practice writing ocean poetry.

Sea Swells *(cont.)*

Closing

Encourage the students to write a poem in free verse (i.e., not following a specific form). Have the students read aloud one of the poems they wrote.

Extension

Direct each student to choose one of his or her poems to illustrate on colored construction paper. The student should copy the poem neatly on lined paper, trim the poem, and place it on the scrapbook page. He or she may include photographs, drawings, and conversation balloons, as well as construction-paper scraps, border templates, and fancy scissors, to create the scrapbook page.

Sea

By Justin V.

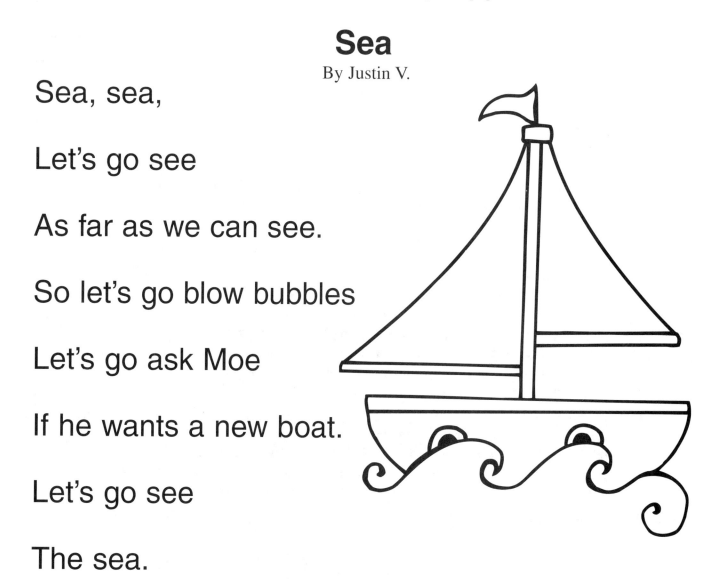

Sea, sea,

Let's go see

As far as we can see.

So let's go blow bubbles

Let's go ask Moe

If he wants a new boat.

Let's go see

The sea.

Rhythm Has Many Forms

Haiku

_____

(five syllables)

_____

(seven syllables)

_____

(five syllables)

Couplets

_____ A

_____ A

_____ B

_____ B

Cinquain

_____
noun

_____   _____
adjective   adjective

_____, _____, _____
verb   verb   verb

_____
(statement of four words)

_____
noun

Free Verse

There will not be . . .

_____

It does not have to be . . .

_____

But there will be . . .

_____,

_____,

and

_____

_____

_____.

(closing sentence)

"What If . . . ?"

Objective

Given a sample and the opportunity to ask questions, the students will engage in the process of thinking "What if . . . ?" to write an expressive composition.

Materials

- white board, overhead projector, or chart paper and marker
- short video clip of a storm at sea or magazine pictures depicting storms at sea
- "Scuba Diving" (page 55)
- hole punch, metal brads
- "Lost at Sea!" (page 56), one copy per student (optional)
- colored construction paper, 9" x 12" (23 cm x 30 cm), one sheet per student (optional)
- markers or colored pencils (optional)

Opening

Show the video clip to the class or show the class a series of magazine pictures to depict a storm at sea. Engage the class in a discussion about how the situation might have ended differently if various factors had been different. Ask the question, "What would have happened if . . . ?"

Directions

1. Tell the students that an important aspect of Fluency is the process of thinking, "What would happen if . . . ?" When writers ask themselves that question at every turning point in a story, they create a process, or sequence of events, that keeps the story flowing smoothly. Even when writing a nonfiction piece, writers should ask themselves, "What comes next?"

2. Read aloud "Scuba Diving" (page 55). After you read the story, ask the students questions such as, "What would have happened if the older brother realized he didn't have everybody? What could have happened when he tried to look for Anna? What would have happened if Anna had not been left behind? Would something else have happened to keep the story interesting? What could that have been? What would have happened if Anna had found the boat right away? What would have happened if they hadn't come to find Anna after three days? What might happen to Anna if she decided to go scuba diving again?"

3. Divide the students into small groups. Have each student write an opening sentence for a "Lost at Sea!" story. Students will then hand their paper to the next person in the group. That person will ask himself, "What happens next?" or "What would happen if . . . ?" The student then writes one or two more sentences for the story. Students continue to pass papers around until each person has the paper he or she started with. Students may then share the stories with one another and discuss other "What if . . . ?" possibilities.

"What If . . . ?" *(cont.)*

Closing

Have the students write a journal entry as if they were lost at sea. They should remember to write with a natural rhythm, as if they were talking to someone, and use words to match the mood of the writing.

Extension

Have the students create a wheel book using their "Lost at Sea!" stories or journal entries. Distribute copies of "Lost at Sea!" (page 56) and construction paper. Students will write a part of their story on each of the eight sections; then they will cut out the circle. Students will trace the circle onto colored construction paper and cut it out; then they will punch a hole in the center of each circle, match the holes, and place a brad in the center to connect the two circles. Finally, the students will cut a pie-shaped wedge from the cover (to show one section of the writing at a time). Students should write the title of their story and their name on the cover of the wheel book. They may decorate the cover if desired.

Scuba Diving

by Brianna K.

Once upon a time, there was a girl who loved scuba diving. Her name was Anna. She had two sisters who also really liked scuba diving. They decided to go out scuba diving, so their older brother took them. Just as they got out of the water, Anna got left behind. Their older brother thought that he had everybody. No, not everybody. When Anna was done scuba diving she could not find the boat. She looked and she looked, but she had no luck. She survived three days and three nights until someone came after her. After that happened, she never ever went scuba diving again!

Lost at Sea!

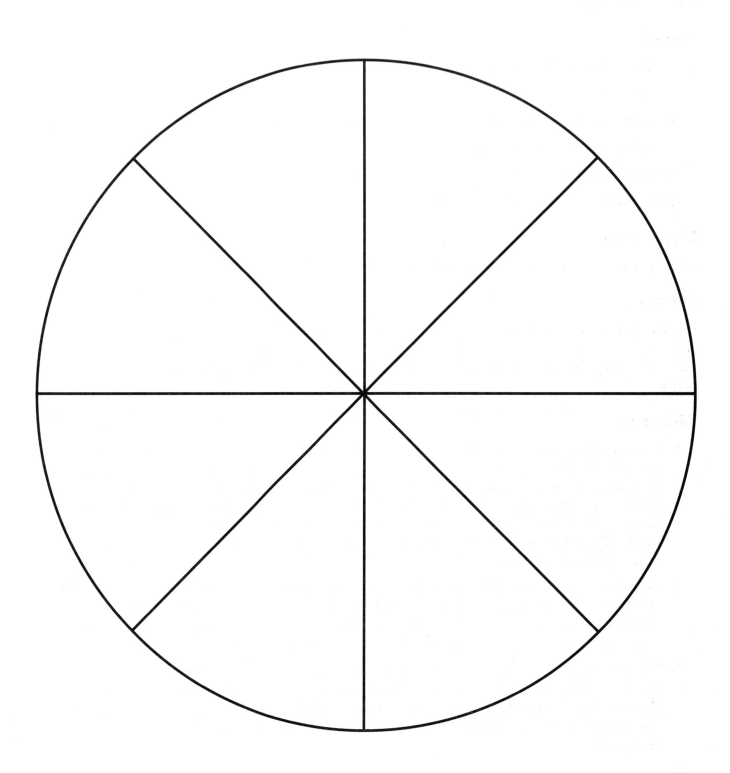

Putting It All Together

Objective

Given a review of the characteristics of the Fluency trait, the students will plan, write, illustrate, and present a complete story to the class.

Materials

- "Three Dolphins" (page 58)
- pictures of the ocean (e.g., photographs, magazine pictures)
- "One Thing Leads to Another" (page 59), one copy per student
- sticky notes, at least three per student
- white construction paper, 9" x 12" (23 cm x 30 cm), one sheet per student (optional)
- colored pencils or crayons (optional)

Preparation

Post the ocean pictures so that the students can view the pictures later in the lesson.

Opening

Ask the students to help review the characteristics of the Fluency trait. Refer the students to the "Fluency" poster (page 44), if necessary. Have the students share what they have learned and how each trait studied thus far builds on the previous traits (i.e., how each trait incorporates characteristics from previous traits).

Directions

1. Explain that for writing to flow smoothly, the ideas should begin purposefully and connect to one another. The author's purpose, or reason for writing, should be evident. Ideas should join together smoothly so that the writing makes sense and readers can follow the story easily. Effective writing also passes the "read-aloud" test. That is, the writing has natural rhythm and flows smoothly enough that a reader can read the writing aloud, without stumbling over the words. The writing makes sense when read aloud, without readers having to repeat sentences to understand what they read.

2. Read aloud "Three Dolphins" (page 58). Discuss in what ways the writing passes the "read-aloud" test. Ask the students what they think the author's purpose was for writing the story. How did ideas connect with one another? Were there sentences that were unnecessary to the story? Were there places where it seemed something important had been left out?

3. Distribute copies of "One Thing Leads to Another" (page 59). Go over the graphic organizer with the class, clarifying and answering questions as necessary. Refer the students to the posted ocean pictures. Tell the class they may use the pictures to help them think of ideas for an ocean story. Have the students use page 59 to plan a complete story about the ocean; then have them write an ocean story.

Putting It All Together *(cont.)*

Closing

Allow time for the students to read their ocean stories to the class. If you have a large class or limited time, divide the students into smaller groups to read their stories. As the students read, their classmates should evaluate the stories. Direct the students to write the comments on sticky notes. They may consider how well the story makes sense, whether the writing flows smoothly, and how well it passes the "read-aloud" test. Encourage the students to write positive comments; if a student needs to improve his or her writing, tell the students to write one positive comment and then a positive way in which the student could revise the writing.

Extension

Have the students illustrate their stories on white construction paper using colored pencils or crayons. Encourage the students to try different techniques to achieve desired effects. Bind the stories and illustrations in a class book.

Three Dolphins

by Geneva F.

Once upon a time, there were three dolphins named Jamie, Jessica, and Jacklyn. They lived in a small lake by the ocean called Swan Lake. It had a waterfall with a waterslide, and it had rocks and pretty mermaids. It had sparkling water. It was fantastic! There was a unicorn, Pegasus, who flew all over the beautiful, sunny sky.

They loved to play in the fountain in the middle of the lake. They had a wonderful time. When it was time to go to bed, the mermaids would tell stories to the dolphins. When it was feeding time, they went to the ocean nearby and got some things to eat.

One day an otter was swimming in their territory. They got mad and they tried to get revenge, but it didn't work so they decided to ask him to stop. He didn't. When they were nice to him, he didn't do it anymore.

One Thing Leads to Another

Words I could use to match the mood or
add meaning:

_____

_____

_____

_____

_____

Characters:

_____

_____

_____

What happens in my story?

Voice

As students learn about the trait of Fluency, they begin to learn about writing style. The Voice trait focuses specifically on a writer's individual style. An effective piece of writing that exhibits aspects of the Voice trait will sound like a particular person wrote it. Therefore, writing that has characteristics of Voice will also be fluent; it will have natural rhythm. The author's personality comes through in the writing. Authors develop their own unique style by writing from their thoughts and feelings.

Effective writers focus on their audience; they write to the reader. They want to call attention to the writing and draw the reader in. To do this, authors will write honestly, sincerely, and with confidence. As they write based on their own experiences and knowledge of themselves, writers will have the ability to bring the topic to life.

Students will continue to practice expanding their perspectives, as well as read sample pieces written from another person's point of view. They will identify elements of the Voice trait in written samples and begin to develop their own style by writing reflections and personal correspondence.

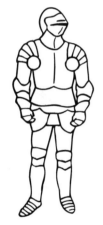 

  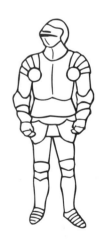

Voice

- sound like a particular person wrote the piece

- allow reader to sense a real person

- author's personality comes through in the writing

- writing comes from author's thoughts and feelings

- natural rhythm

- call attention to the writing

- write sincerely, with confidence

- write to the reader; stay focused on the audience

- convey honesty

- bring the topic to life

- write out of knowing yourself

Getting to Know Jellanos

Objective

Given sample diary entries, the students will analyze the thoughts and feelings of a character.

Materials

- white board, overhead projector, or chart paper and marker
- "Voice" poster (page 61), one copy for display
- "Dear Journal" (page 63), one copy per student
- "A Writer's Style" (page 64), one copy per student
- classroom resources about medieval times (optional)
- white butcher paper, 3–4 feet (90 cm or 120 cm) per group (optional)
- colored pencils, crayons, chalk, or oil pastels (optional)

Preparation

Enlarge the "Voice" poster (page 61) for display.

Opening

Draw the students' attention to the "Voice" poster (page 61). Just as people sound differently when they speak, authors use individual voices in their writing. Have different student volunteers say the same phrase for the class. Ask the students how each person's personality comes through in the way he or she speaks. Discuss how an author's personality can come through in writing.

Directions

1. Continue a discussion on how writing can exhibit qualities of the Voice trait. As writers allow their personality to show in their writing, they will also include their thoughts and feelings. Writers may also express their attitudes and opinions about the topic as they write.

2. Distribute copies of "Dear Journal" (page 63). Have a student volunteer read it aloud. Ask the students to visualize the author as they listen. What does the person look like? What are his personality traits (e.g., quiet, loud, honest, lazy, hardworking, friendly)?

3. Brainstorm and make a class list of thoughts, feelings, and attitudes an author might express.

4. Distribute copies of "A Writer's Style" (page 64). Have the students silently read "Dear Journal" (page 63). They will refer to this sample journal to complete page 64.

Closing

Have the students pretend to be Jellanos. They will write the next day of his journal entries. Students may refer to classroom resources about medieval times for ideas.

Getting to Know Jellanos *(cont.)*

Extension

Divide the students into small groups. Have the students refer to "Dear Journal" (page 63). They may also use classroom resources for ideas. Students will create a mural to depict the sequence of days in Jellanos' life (i.e., their mural will be like a tapestry showing the story of Jellanos' life). Encourage the students to include texture in their drawings to make the mural appear more lifelike.

Dear Journal
by Justin V.

Day 1

Today the king just announced a new knight, and the plan of war in the east. I got a new job as stable boy. I worked and earned five pieces of gold. I can buy a stick and net and go fish for my dinner. I will talk to my brother Andea and he will make another dagger to cut the fish.

Day 2

Yesterday I got a new stick and net. I caught a three-pound fish and Andea made me a dagger. I earned thirty-one pieces of gold. I have to go, Master Genesalo calls me!

Jellanos

A Writer's Style

1. List any specific words the author used to show his personality.

   _____

   _____

   _____

   _____

   _____

2. What words or phrases did the writer use to show his thoughts and feelings?

   _____

   _____

   _____

   _____

   _____

3. What is the author's attitude in this piece? How can you tell?

   _____

   _____

   _____

   _____

   _____

4. Is the writing honest? yes _____ no _____

5. Does the author express ideas clearly? yes _____ no _____

6. Is the writing original? yes _____ no _____

Stepping Back in Time

Objective

Given a discussion about characteristics of people, the students will read a descriptive paragraph and respond by pretending to be that character.

Materials

- white board, overhead projector, or chart paper and marker
- photographs or magazine pictures of people
- "Middle Ages" (page 66)
- "Becoming Real" (page 67), one copy per student
- pictures depicting medieval times (optional)
- classroom resources about medieval times (optional)
- costumes and other props for role-play (optional)

Opening

Show the students photographs or pictures of people. Have the students list characteristics of people. Make a chart on the white board with category headings such as: eyes, hair, skin, frame (e.g., height, weight), temperament (e.g., mild, rough, loud), and other personality traits. For each picture, ask the students to describe the person and complete the chart accordingly.

Directions

1. Explain that each picture represents an individual person. Writing that exhibits qualities of the Voice trait sounds like a particular person wrote it. The writer allows the reader to sense a real person. Authors accomplish this by including their thoughts, feelings, attitudes, opinions, and other aspects of their own personality in their writing. They may also write from a specific point of view: as a narrator or as the main character. A writer may pretend to be all-knowing or he or she may limit information to what just one character might be able to see and know. Remind the students that it is important to maintain the same point of view throughout one written piece.

2. Read aloud "Middle Ages" (page 66). As you read, have the students draw a picture of the narrator of the piece.

3. Distribute copies of "Becoming Real" (page 67). Read aloud "Middle Ages" (page 66) again and ask the students to consider the type of person who narrated the piece. Have the students give the character a name and pretend to be that person as they complete page 67. Students may also complete their drawing, adding color and other details.

4. Have the students use their idea pages and drawings to write a descriptive paragraph. They will describe the narrator of "Middle Ages" (page 66).

Stepping Back in Time *(cont.)*

Closing

Read a selection of the students' descriptive paragraphs anonymously. You might have students show "thumbs up, thumbs down" to evaluate how well each author described the character.

Extension

Have the students role-play a scene from a medieval character's life. For example, the character might participate in a jousting tournament. Refer the students to classroom resources about medieval times, if you have them available.

Middle Ages

by Trey U.

A long time ago, there was a time period called "medieval times." In medieval times, there were knights, castles, and more. Medieval means "Middle Ages." It was very scary! Most castles were in Rome, England, and Scotland. There were lots of wars. Dragons were not real; they were just imaginary.

Becoming Real

Hello, my [character's] name is _____.

I am _____ and I have _____ hair.
     describe height   color

People say my eyes are _____ and _____.
                   color   shape

I think I am _____, _____, and _____.
                personality traits

My unique features include:

_____

color or type of skin

_____

birthmarks or other unique qualities

_____

how I treat other people

I live in this kind of place: _____

Other words people would use to describe me:

_____

_____

_____

_____

Calling My Reader

Objective

Given further instruction in the qualities of the Voice trait, the students will write an advertisement that focuses a reader's attention on the writing.

Materials

- white board, overhead projector, or chart paper and marker
- sample magazine advertisements
- "Wonderful Armor" (page 69), one copy for display
- "My Wares Are Wonderful" (page 70), one copy per student
- felt and fabric trims (e.g., sequins, buttons, rickrack, ribbon) (optional)
- fabric scissors and glue (optional)

Preparation

- Enlarge "Wonderful Armor" (page 69) for display.

Opening

Show the students the sample advertisements. Ask the students how the authors called attention to their writing. What words or phrases did they use to help focus the reader's interest? How did they get the reader to consider and concentrate on their work?

Directions

1. Tell the students that important aspects of the Voice trait include writing to the reader and staying focused on the audience. Writers want to call attention to their writing, and one way they can do this is to keep the audience in mind as they write. Writers want to address their words and thoughts directly to the reader. The reader becomes the focus of the writer's thoughts and the writing itself becomes the focus of the reader's activity or interest; the written piece becomes a means of communication or conversation between the reader and the writer. Show the students "Wonderful Armor" (page 69). Ask them how this advertisement focuses on the reader and his or her interest.

2. Distribute copies of "My Wares Are Wonderful" (page 70). Tell the class that often during the Middle Ages, craftsmen formed guilds. Craftsmen made various items to sell as their trade, or business, to make money. Trades included blacksmiths, bakers, tailors, candle makers, weavers, and carpenters. Have the students choose a trade and complete page 70, describing the item they have for sale.

3. Remind the students that word of mouth was the main way people could advertise what they had for sale; TV and radio did not exist and newspapers were scarce. The crier would want to call attention to what he had to say, and he would also be aware of his audience, the passersby on the street. Have the students write a jingle they could sing to attract people to their shop.

Calling My Reader *(cont.)*

Closing

Divide the students into small groups. Have the students take turns presenting the jingles within their group. As they listen, group members should write questions about the items their classmates have for sale. Once each person has had a turn to read his or her jingle, the other students may ask and respond to the questions.

Extension

Students may use felt and fabric trim to create a banner for their trade. Banners should call attention to the craft or trade advertised and focus on the audience. If more than one student chooses a given trade, those students could work in pairs to create a banner for their shop. Display the banners as part of a medieval unit of study, if desired.

Wonderful Armor
by Caleb V.

Oh, buy my wonderful, wonderful, wonderful

armor, armor, armor.

I'm sure, I'm sure

you'll like it, you'll like it.

I'm sure you will.

You probably don't want to

get hurt, hurt, hurt.

That's the end of that.

My Wares Are Wonderful

My special experience or training to make this item:

_____

_____

_____

_____

_____

Craft or other item for sale:

_____

_____

Why my product is better than someone else's:

_____

_____

_____

_____

Ways my product may be used to make the customer's life better:

_____

_____

_____

_____

_____

Price of the item:

_____

_____

Other information for the buyer:

_____

_____

_____

_____

_____

Come Join the Quest

Objective

Given instruction in persuasive writing, the students will practice writing sincerely and with confidence by writing a persuasive brochure.

Materials

- "Seeking Wisdom and Knowledge" (page 73), one copy per student
- colored pencils, two different colors per student
- "Travel Guide" (page 74), one copy per student
- markers and magazine pictures (optional)
- published samples of persuasive writing (optional)
- pictures depicting medieval times (optional)
- white construction paper, 12" x 18" (30 cm x 45 cm), one sheet per student (optional)

Opening

Ask the students to define *persuasive writing*. Explain that this is a type of writing in which the author tries to convince the reader to believe something is true or to behave in a certain way. You might want to read one or two samples of persuasive writing to the class.

Directions

1. Draw the students' attention to the "Voice" poster (page 61). Point out that writers who include aspects of the Voice trait show honesty in their writing, write out of knowing themselves first, and write sincerely and with confidence. Discuss the fact that when writers know their strengths and weaknesses and their own personality traits, they can then write with certainty about chosen topics. Believing in themselves and their work gives writers confidence so they can write with assurance. This gives the writing strength, which will attract the reader.

2. Distribute copies of "Seeking Wisdom and Knowledge" (page 73). Have the students use colored pencils to emphasize various aspects of the Voice trait. They should use one color to underline words or phrases that persuade or convince the reader. Students should use the other color to mark which words or phrases in which the writer shows honesty, self-knowledge, sincerity, and confidence.

3. Distribute copies of "Travel Guide" (page 74). Tell the students they will use this page to plan a brochure. The brochure will convince other people to join them on their quest.

   Explain to the students that during the Middle Ages, people often took a quest or journey in search of meaning for their lives. They would travel together in groups for companionship and safety.

Come Join the Quest *(cont.)*

Closing

Have the students use "Travel Guide" (page 74) to create a brochure. Their brochure should include a paragraph written with honesty, sincerity, and confidence, asserting that this journey is a good idea. You may want the students to create a rough draft first. Remind the students to write to their readers and focus on their audience. You may choose to have the students use markers and magazine pictures to decorate their brochures.

Extension

Students may create a map to show where they will travel on their quest. Distribute white construction paper to the students. They should draw and label the map and include landforms and other identifying landmarks. (This may be a fictional country.)

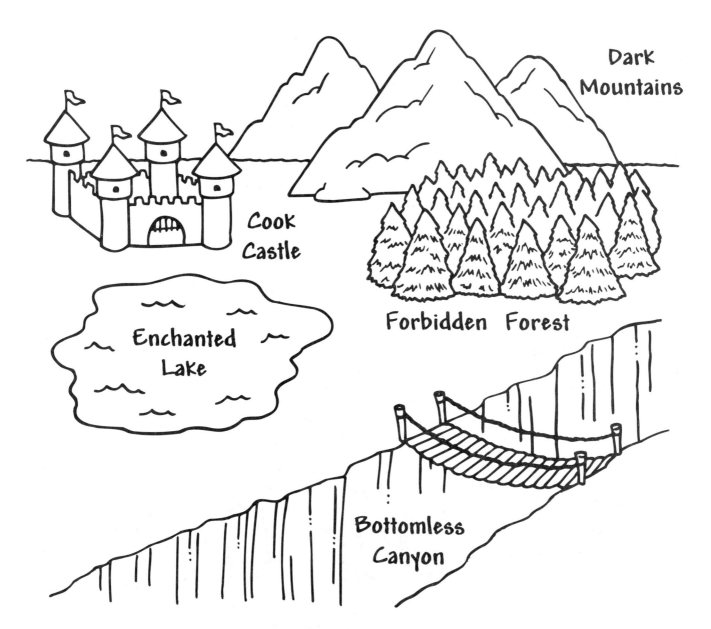

Seeking Wisdom and Knowledge

by Kenneth M.

Knowledge is the key that unlocks any physical door. To unlock other parts of one's life—to truly learn all one can, one must learn more than simple facts. A quest has been offered as a way to learn more, experience more, and meet new people.

A large company will begin a quest to Rome. You are a lucky member who is invited! This is a good way to learn what cannot be taught by books. Do you want to learn how to survive? to fish? This quest will teach not only these things, but also about relationships and more! Every night people will learn from others. The more people who join the quest, the more wisdom to be offered!

Experience life as well! Stop reading books, and begin a life journey that will revive you physically, mentally, and spiritually. Finally, meet others and learn. Invest in others, and share experiences and various emotions. If you are in need of danger, love, or any wild excitement, this is for you!

Rome

Join Our Quest

Travel Guide

1. Where will you go on your quest?

   _____

   _____

   _____

2. How long will it take to get there?

   _____

   _____

   _____

3. How will you travel? Do you have to go across land or water?

   _____

   _____

   _____

4. Why are you making this journey?

   _____

   _____

   _____

5. What are you seeking or hoping to find?

   _____

   _____

   _____

6. What kind of people would you like to have with you on your journey? Do you need people who have particular skills (e.g., people who can weave cloth, people who can hunt well)?

   _____

   _____

   _____

7. What benefits will your traveling companions receive from going with you on this journey?

   _____

   _____

   _____

Bringing Writing to Life

Objective

Given a review of the characteristics of the Voice trait, the students will write an article that includes details about a historical time period.

Materials

- "Medieval Times" (page 77), one copy per student
- "This Is News!" (page 78), one copy per student
- "My Audience" (page 79), one copy per student
- modeling clay, container (optional)
- paint, fabric scraps, twigs and other small items for props (optional)

Preparation

If students will complete the Extension activity and commercial modeling clay is not available, make simple salt dough to use as clay.

Salt Dough

2 cups (475 mL) self-rising flour
2 tablespoons (30 mL) salt
2 tablespoons (30 mL) alum
2 tablespoons (30 mL) cooking oil
$1\frac{1}{4}$ cups (300 mL) boiling water
food coloring (optional)

Mix and knead, adding food coloring if desired.
Store the dough in a sealed, air-tight container.

Opening

Review with the class the "Voice" poster (page 61). Have the students briefly define and explain each aspect. Ask the students how practicing qualities of the Voice trait has helped them in their writing.

Directions

1. Ask the students what they think it means to "bring the topic to life." Discuss how effective writing shows action and energy. An author can bring writing to life by showing enthusiasm and excitement in the writing so that the characters and action feel alive. Students can exhibit this aspect of the Voice trait by remembering to include characteristics of other traits (e.g., using action verbs as learned in studying the Word Choice trait).

Bringing Writing to Life *(cont.)*

Directions *(cont.)*

2. Distribute copies of "Medieval Times" (page 77) and "This Is News!" (page 78). Explain that the students will read a story that has been written in a similar way to a news article. They will use page 78 to identify major points of information in the story: *who, what, where, when, why*, and *how*. Have the students read "Medieval Times" (page 77). Then instruct them to write a brief statement, identifying each component, and draw a picture to portray the scene as they imagine it.

3. Have the students share their responses or drawings with other classmates. Discuss the story so that everyone has a mental picture of the scenes.

4. Distribute copies of "My Audience" (page 79). Have the students use the sheet to plan a news article. They may write about an event that might have happened during the Middle Ages, perhaps related to another writing exercise they have completed during the Voice Unit. Encourage the students to remember to focus on their audience and give careful thought to who would read the article—perhaps a person from that time period. Their article should include information of interest to the reader.

Closing

Have the students compile their news articles into a "gazette" that might be posted around a small medieval community. You may want the students to give feedback to each other to clarify their news articles and check for specific aspects of the Voice trait. If so, have the students write a final copy before publishing in the class gazette.

Extension

Students may use modeling clay to bring the event depicted in their news article to life. They may include small items as props to enhance the scene.

Medieval Times
by Justin V.

Once there was a knight who traveled with some men to a town called Lincolnshire.

One of the men said, "We are sorely afraid for our lives. The Black Death has been reported in Lincolnshire. That town is only 20 miles from here! I am not going if I'm going to die."

The knight agreed. On their way back, they saw 29 men and 10 knights. At the knight's command, his men went back and saved their town. He became a champion. He married the princess and together they had a son.

The son grew up wanting to be like his dad. He wanted to be a knight, but he became a blacksmith when he was 29. He was making a breastplate when he heard 24 knights charging after him. They stopped him and gave him a note that said, "We want you to become a knight."

He jumped for joy on his table and ran to the king. He said, "I want to become that knight."

The king said, "You start training at 2:30 p.m. today." It was 2:28 p.m., so he ran to the training grounds and trained for three years.

He won 290 challenges and 2 wars, just like his father. His servant was scarred while in battle, but he came back alive.

This Is News!

Who	What

Where	When

Why	How

My Audience

1. Who will read my news article?

_____

_____

2. What information should I include that would be interesting to my audience?

_____

_____

_____

3. What event happened that I want people to know about?

_____

_____

4. When does this event take place?

_____

_____

5. Where does this event take place?

_____

_____

6. Why is this news important?

_____

_____

_____

7. How is this news important to my reader?

_____

_____

_____

8. How might the reader react to this news?

_____

_____

_____

Organization

As students learn to incorporate the Organization trait in their writing, they begin to view the whole picture. Effective writing has a logical order and sequence with clear direction and purpose. It does not confuse the reader. Rather, writing which displays qualities of organization guides the reader through the writing, leading to the main point. Writers who incorporate the characteristics of the Organization trait include an introduction that captures the reader's attention and conclude the piece by making the reader think. Organized writing flows smoothly, with transitions that tie together.

Students will practice the characteristics of this trait by identifying elements of organization in a written sample piece. They will also learn about paragraph structure and write their own paragraphs. The teacher will introduce story elements to the students and give them opportunities to practice outlining a story, identifying story elements, and writing a complete story. As students write their own stories, they will focus on including appropriate pacing and transitions in their writing.

Organization

- has attention-getting introduction

- conclusion makes the reader think

- logical order and sequence

- appropriate pacing

- flows smoothly

- transitions tie together

- path leads reader to the main point

- guides reader through the writing

- clear direction and purpose

- links back to main idea

Investigating Effective Writing

Objective

Given an introduction to the Organization trait, the students will investigate a writing sample for specific aspects of the trait.

Materials

- white board, overhead projector, or chart paper and marker
- "Organization" poster (page 81), one copy for display
- newspaper or magazine articles
- "Earthquake!" (page 83), one copy per student
- "A Detective Kit" (page 84), one or two copies per student
- "Keys to Effective Writing" (page 85), two copies per student (optional)
- wire hangers, hole punch, string (optional)

Preparation

Enlarge the "Organization" poster (page 81) for display.

Opening

Tell the students that starting with the Organization trait, they will begin to put the pieces of their writing together to form a whole picture. They will assemble tools and learn strategies to help them.

Directions

1. Show the students the "Organization" poster (page 81). Based on previous lessons, ask the students what they think is meant by the term "attention-getting introduction." Explain that not only do writers want to call attention to their writing, they want to hook the reader right away and capture his or her interest. Doing so will ensure that readers will keep reading the writing, rather than putting it down.

2. Point out also that effective writing has a conclusion that makes the reader think. The writer wants to end the piece in such a way that it leaves the reader feeling satisfied. However, there is still the possibility that the story could continue or, in a nonfiction piece, that there could be additional information.

3. Show the students the sample newspaper or magazine articles. Have the students identify especially interesting opening sentences. Ask the students to notice what catches their attention in an opening sentence or introduction. Are there particular words or phrases? Does the author state the topic right away or does he or she use a technique, such as asking a question or stating a quote, to get the reader's attention?

Investigating Effective Writing *(cont.)*

Directions *(cont.)*

4. Ask the students which conclusions leave them feeling especially satisfied. Do they feel that the story could possibly go on, yet has reached an adequate ending? Are there words or phrases that make it seem as if the story has reached an end?

5. Tell the students that overall, the Organization trait focuses on including logical structure and enough information to help the reader understand the writing. Distribute copies of "Earthquake!" (page 83). Tell the students that they will read this sample and identify key pieces of information: *who*, *what*, *where*, *when*, *why*, and *how*. They will also take note of the introduction and the conclusion.

6. Give each student a copy of "A Detective Kit" (page 84). Explain that the students will use this page to record the key elements they find in "Earthquake!" (page 83).

Closing

Have the students use the same journalistic format of including *who*, *what*, *where*, *when*, *why*, and *how* to write their own brief article as if they were a newspaper reporter investigating a natural disaster. If desired, give the students a second copy of "Detective Kit" (page 84) to plan their article. You may wish to have a class discussion about types of natural disasters such as volcanoes, earthquakes, tsunamis, and hurricanes. This may tie in with any current events or news articles the class has read recently.

Extension

Have the students make a mobile. Distribute two copies of "Keys to Effective Writing" to each student. Have the students cut out the keys. On each key, they should write one of the characteristics of the Organization trait. (Students may color or decorate the keys before cutting them out and assembling the mobile.) Have the students punch a hole in each key and assemble the mobile by attaching the keys to the hanger with string.

Earthquake!

by Faith U.

There was a huge earthquake in South Asia. Many officials are scared that as many as 40,000 people were killed by the earthquake. This earthquake happened on October 8, 2005, at 8:50 A.M. I bet a lot of people are sad because part of their family died.

A Detective Kit

Why

What

Who

How

When

Where

Keys to Effective Writing

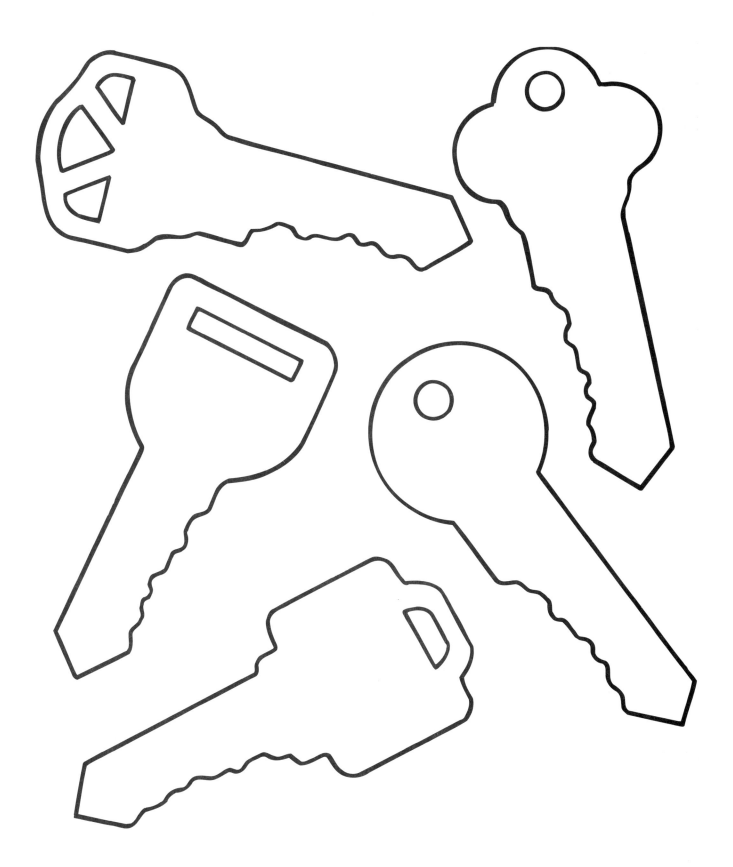

Step by Step

Objective

Given pictorial scenes of an event, the students will make a timeline showing the sequence of events using transitions.

Materials

- white board, overhead projector, or chart paper and colored marker
- video of volcanic eruption or magazine pictures showing a volcanic eruption (available from National Geographic)
- "Timeline" (page 87), one copy for display
- "Sequencing Events" (page 88), one copy per student
- classroom resources (e.g., trade books, magazine articles) about volcanoes or other natural disasters

Preparation

Enlarge "Timeline" (page 87) for display.

Opening

Show the class the video or magazine pictures of a volcanic eruption. Ask the students if a volcanic eruption or other natural disaster has a sequence of events.

Directions

1. Discuss the concept that organized writing contains a logical order and sequence of events. That is, the actions in a piece of writing happen in a way that makes sense from beginning to end. The reader is able to follow the events, without becoming confused, as he or she reads.
2. Show the students "Timeline" (page 87). Point out features of a timeline (e.g., dates in chronological order).
3. Have the students also identify any transition words that are used. Underline these words with a colored marker. Explain that transition words lead the reader from one sentence or thought to the next.
4. Distribute copies of "Sequencing Events" (page 88). Have the students create a timeline showing major events that occur when a natural disaster happens. Encourage the students to include details and think about the order of the events.

Closing

Photocopy the students' completed timelines (page 88). Have the students cut apart the copy of their timeline. They will give the cut pieces to a partner and have their partner re-assemble the timeline in the correct order. Students may discuss with each other aspects of sequencing events and which words helped to put the events in the correct order.

Extension

Have the students use their timelines as a reference to make a pictorial mural of the events that occur in a natural disaster. The mural may be displayed as part of a social studies or science unit.

Timeline

by Dallas G.

Erupts

First the volcano would erupt in boiling lava.

Scramble

There would be a scramble for cars, trucks, and other transportation.

Destroyed Homes

Last, there would be tons of homes destroyed.

Alert

Then officials would tell you to evacuate.

Lost Lives

There are sometimes casualties (deaths).

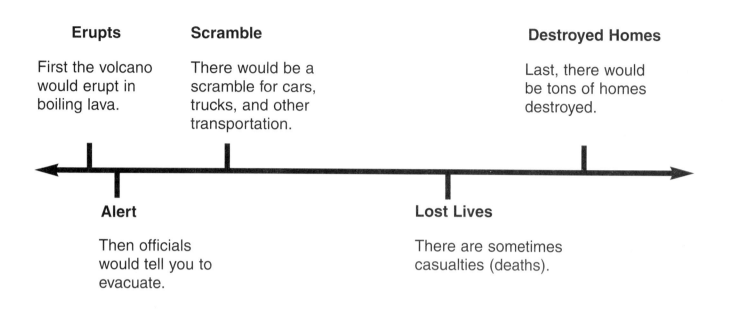

Sequencing Events

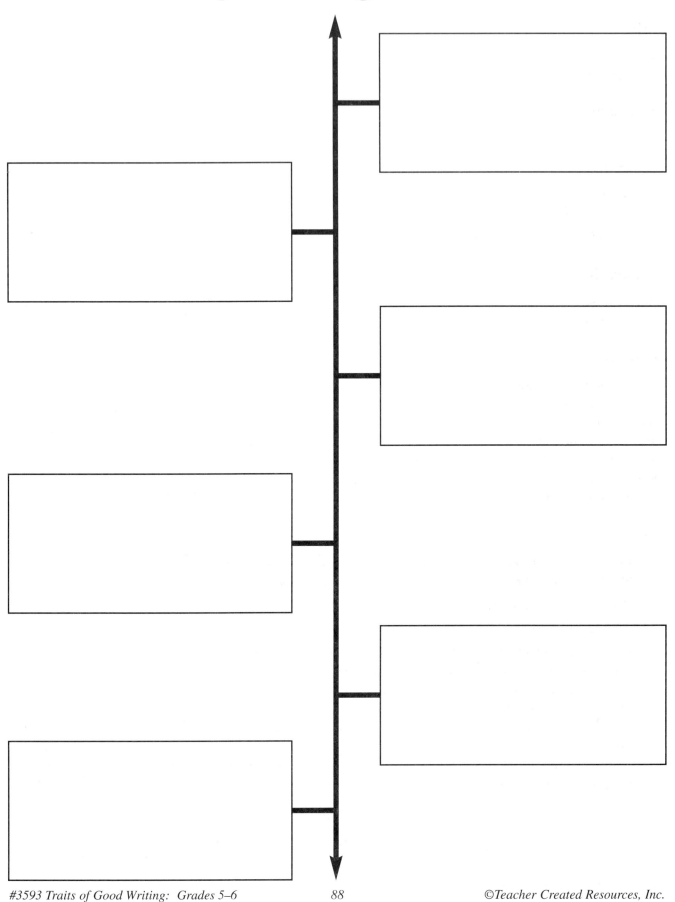

Perfect Paragraphs

Objective

Given a review of paragraph structure, the students will write and evaluate paragraphs by participating in a round-robin activity.

Materials

- white board, overhead projector, or chart paper and marker
- "Volcanoes" (page 90)
- white construction paper, 12" x 18" (30 cm x 45 cm), two sheets cut into six 4" x 18" (10 cm x 45 cm) strips
- "One Sentence at a Time" (page 91), one copy per student

Preparation

Write each sentence of "Volcanoes" (page 90) on a separate strip of white construction paper, or enlarge the sentences and cut them into strips.

Opening

Select student volunteers to hold up the sentence strips for the class to see. Each student should hold one strip; the students should stand in order so that the paragraph reads from left to right. Have volunteers read the strips aloud. Tell the class that these sentences form a complete paragraph. Ask the students to identify the *topic sentence*, or a sentence that tells what the paragraph is about. Have another student identify the *closing*, or ending sentence. Tell the students that the other sentences in the paragraph, those between the beginning sentence and the ending sentence, are *body sentences*. These sentences contain details about the topic of the paragraph.

Directions

1. Read aloud "Volcanoes" (page 90) again. Have the students identify specific details within the paragraph. Discuss how the paragraph fits together as a whole unit of writing.

2. Distribute copies of "One Sentence at a Time" (page 91). Tell the students they will practice writing paragraphs by writing one sentence at a time.

3. Divide the students into small groups. Have each student think of a topic about which to write a paragraph. He or she should write a topic sentence for the paragraph on #1 on page 91. Students will then pass their paper to the next person in their group. Each person will read the topic sentence their classmate wrote and then write a sentence telling a detail about that topic on #2. Students continue to pass papers around the group, writing one sentence on each paper on #3 and #4. During the last turn, students should write a concluding sentence for the paragraph on #5. After a student writes a sentence on page 91, the student should write his or her initials in the margin by that sentence.

Perfect Paragraphs *(cont.)*

Closing

Have the students take turns reading aloud the paragraphs to the group. Group members should evaluate how well the paragraphs stay on topic and fit together as a whole. Students may give the paragraphs a number rating from one to five, with one as a score for a "choppy paragraph" that does not stay on topic to five as a score for the "perfect paragraph," one which meets all criteria discussed during the lesson.

Extension

List on the white board several topics of current interest about which students could write paragraphs. Have the students select a topic and write one complete paragraph about that topic. Encourage the students to include details in the body sentences of their paragraph.

Volcanoes

by Marie B.

Mountains that erupt are called *volcanoes*.

Vents in Earth's crust allow hot gases and magma to escape.

Lava, rock, and soil accumulate to form a volcano.

When enough pressure builds up within the mountain, the volcano will erupt.

During an eruption, lava, steam, rocks, and ash, or a combination of all of these, burst forth from the mountain.

The eruption leaves a crack in the volcano, allowing steam and hot gases to escape until sediment and pressure build up again.

One Sentence at a Time

1. Select a topic for your paragraph. Write a topic sentence telling what the paragraph will be about.

_____

_____

_____

2. Write the next sentence for the paragraph. Include at least one detail or example about the topic.

_____

_____

_____

3. Write another sentence for the paragraph. Include one more detail about the topic or expand on the ideas written in the previous sentence.

_____

_____

_____

4. Write a third sentence about the topic. Include more details, an example, or expand on the sentences previously written.

_____

_____

_____

5. Write a concluding, or ending, sentence for the paragraph. This sentence should refer back to the main topic in some way or restate the topic.

_____

_____

_____

Pathway to Rescue

Objective

Given a review of story elements, the students will draw pictures to depict a story and write sentences related to the pictures.

Materials

- "Marshmallow Eruption!" (page 93), one copy per student
- classroom resources about volcanoes (e.g., books, magazines, posters, USGS brochures)
- colored pencils or crayons
- "A Path Through the Story" (page 94), two copies per student
- overhead projector and markers (optional)
- index cards, ten per group (optional)

Opening

Have the students consider their favorite stories. Ask them what makes a particular story their favorite. Guide the students in a discussion about stories that make sense, lead the reader through to the main point, have a logical order or sequence, and include all necessary information to make a complete story.

Directions

1. Review with the students the "Organization Poster" (page 81). Explain that writing with these qualities guides the reader by providing a path through the writing. The writing makes sense; the reader will not become confused but will follow along and read the piece to the end.

2. Introduce or review the key components of a story: characters, setting (time), setting (place), a problem or conflict (plot), the most important moment (climax), resolution of the problem, dialogue, introduction, and conclusion.

3. Distribute copies of "Marshmallow Eruption!" (page 93). Give each student one copy of "A Path Through the Story" (page 94). Discuss how each sentence corresponds to one or more story elements. Have the students read the sentences on page 93 and write each sentence in the corresponding box on page 94. Ask the students to consider how well the story flows. Will the author need to expand on this outline to write a complete story? Why or why not? Students may write a journal response to these questions on the other side of page 93. If the students have extra time, have them draw pictures to accompany the sentences in "Marshmallow Eruption!" (page 93).

Pathway to Rescue *(cont.)*

Directions *(cont.)*

4. Distribute a second copy of "A Path Through the Story" (page 94). Explain that the students will think of characters, setting, plot, etc., as part of a complete story about a volcano. They will draw pictures to show each aspect of the story. Students will also write sentences to go with their pictures. Demonstrate completing this process using an overhead projector if desired. The students may need to decide on basic components of their story (e.g., characters, setting, plot), before they begin to draw pictures and write sentences. Students should write any ideas and thoughts they have before they draw their pictures. Students may refer to classroom resources about volcanoes to get ideas for their stories.

Closing

Have the students use their pictures and sentences to write a complete story. Allow them to share their stories with the class.

Extension

Divide the students into small groups. Give each group 10 index cards. Students should number their cards 1–10. They will write directions to tell another group how to get from a starting point to an ending point, similar to a trail guide or treasure hunt. Groups may choose to place a small prize at the final destination. Students should take turns writing one direction on each index card. Their directions should include transition words and descriptive words, and follow a logical order or sequence. Explain that the directions will form a path to lead the readers to a final destination point. Have the groups swap their set of cards with another group. Groups will then follow the directions to proceed from the starting point to the ending destination.

Marshmallow Eruption!

by Trey U.

Once there was a volcanic eruption that buried Ompeii. Nobody died. It was not deadly at all.

The mountain erupted marshmallows. They could talk. One was named Fred and the other was named Bob. Fred said, "Ouch, they stabbed me. It's hot. Ouch!" Bob didn't have time to say much of anything.

Someone caught him and put him between two graham crackers with chocolate. This eruption gave more good than bad.

A Path Through the Story

Introduction

Characters

Setting

Problem or Conflict (Plot)

Most Important Moment

Resolution of Problem (Solution)

Conclusion

Why People Write

Objective

Given instruction on the five-paragraph essay and purpose and theme, the students will write a complete essay about an opinion or issue.

Materials

- variety of writing samples (e.g., memo, letter, news article, agenda, list, directions)
- "Stay Informed" (page 97)
- "This Is What I Think" (page 98), one copy per student
- classroom resources used in previous lesson
- "Perfect Paragraphs" (page 89) (optional)
- "Dear Harry" (page 99), one copy per student (optional)

Opening

Show the class a variety of writing samples. Ask the students to list reasons why people write. Discuss some reasons people write: to inform, respond, encourage, tell about something, teach, take notes or remember something, etc. Ask the students what type of writing would go with each reason, or purpose, for writing. Explain that writers often have a message, or theme, they want someone else to hear when they write.

Directions

1. Tell the students that one aspect of Organization is having a clear direction and purpose in writing. If authors do not know what they want to say, their writing will be ineffective, unclear, and not well organized; the reader will become confused and stop reading before the end.

2. Introduce or review the five-paragraph essay. An essay has an introductory paragraph, three main subtopics with one paragraph about each point, and a concluding paragraph. Refer the students to "Perfect Paragraphs" (page 89) for instruction on the structure of individual paragraphs, if necessary.

3. Read aloud "Stay Informed" (page 97). Ask the students to identify the introduction, topic of essay, three subtopics, and conclusion. How does the conclusion refer back to the main point? What details or examples are included in the body of the essay? What is the author's overall message in the essay?

4. Distribute copies of "This Is What I Think" (page 98). Read through the graphic organizer with the class, answering any questions.

5. Explain that the students will write a five-paragraph essay on a specific topic about which they have ideas and opinions. Encourage the students to refer to classroom resources and include facts in their essay. Remind the students to make sure their writing has clear direction and purpose. Their concluding paragraph should link back to the main idea.

Why People Write *(cont.)*

Directions *(cont.)*

6. Tell the class they will write an essay about issues that might arise if scientists were to anticipate a volcanic eruption. Have the students consider the following questions: How large an area should be evacuated? How soon should people be asked to evacuate? Should people be allowed to return to their homes once the apparent danger is past? Who should decide the answers to these questions?

7. Have the students complete "This Is What I Think" (page 98) to plan their essay.

Closing

Have the students use the notes on page 98 to write their essays. Evaluate the student essays based on the criteria in this lesson (see page 95, #2).

Extension

Distribute copies of "Dear Harry" (page 99). Students will read the letter and then write to the author of the letter on page 99. Students may respond specifically to the author's main idea in the letter, his theme or message, or any opinions expressed in the letter.

Stay Informed

by Bob P.

What would you do if a volcano were to erupt close to your home? Think about what would be most important to you. What would you need to know?

The first thing might be what to take with you if you have to leave your house. Make sure everyone in your family is safe. You also want to make sure your pets will be okay.

You would want to know where to go to be safe. Should you go north or south, east or west? The news stations will tell you where you can go. You also want to call your friends and family to let them know where you will be.

Once you get to where you are going, how will you know when you can go home? You might have to wait several days, so it would be a good idea to take some water, food, and blankets. You can read a newspaper or listen to the radio to find out when it is safe to return home.

The most important thing is to be informed. Make a list of local telephone numbers for emergency departments like the police, fire, and other authorities. Being informed is your best way to be safe.

Important
Phone Numbers

Emergency 911
Police 555-4101
Fire 555-1811

This Is What I Think

Plan an essay about actions people should take if scientists were to anticipate a volcanic eruption.

The main thought or idea in my essay is: (author's message or theme)

_____

_____

_____

I am writing the essay for this reason: (the purpose)

_____

_____

_____

The three main things I want to talk about in my essay:

   1. _____

   2. _____

   3. _____

Here are some facts I can include when I talk about each idea:

   1. _____

   2. _____

   3. _____

I want to include these details or examples in each paragraph:

   1. _____

   2. _____

   3. _____

This is how I will end the essay and refer back to my main idea:

_____

_____

_____

Dear Harry

Harry Truman was a man who lived near Mt. St. Helens before the eruption in 1980. He refused to leave the mountain even when others told him he should go to save his own life. Write a response to Kenneth's letter to Harry Truman.

Dear Harry Truman,

If you leave the mountain, you will live. In a few years you can rebuild your lodge. If you stay, I am almost positive you will die and your sister will be very sad.

If you still want to stay, I will tell you that a Hawaiian volcano covered an entire city. If I were you, I'd go.

If you still want to stay, I will tell you that the entire place will turn into a muddy ground. The green trees will crash down and the clear, blue water will turn into muddy water.

But if you go, you can come back in a few years and the place should be back to normal.

Sincerely,

Kenneth M.

Conventions

Students put the pieces together as they worked through the Organization trait and began to consider the whole picture, writing complete stories. They also had the opportunity to begin to consider self-evaluation based on established criteria. The next major step in the writing process is editing. The Conventions trait breaks the huge task of editing into smaller parts, allowing students to practice editing their own and others' work focusing on one factor at a time.

First, students learn proofreading marks which will enable the teacher and class to edit consistently. Students also learn about and practice correct forms of conventions, such as correctly spelling plural and singular forms of nouns, capitalization of place names, punctuation, possessives, and subject-verb agreement. Although students practice characteristics of the Conventions trait mostly by reading and editing samples written by others, they will also continue to work toward editing their own work.

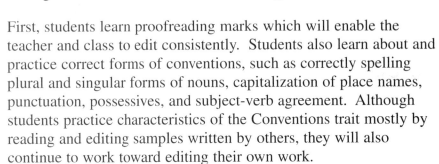

Conventions

- use proofreading marks

- check for correct spelling

- use correct capitalization

- include proper punctuation

- check for grammar and correct word usage

- use action verbs

- check for appropriate paragraphs

- include an appropriate title

The Mark of Excellence

Objective

Given instruction in the use of proofreading marks, the students will practice using the marks to proofread an article.

Materials

- white board, overhead projector, or chart paper and marker
- "Conventions" poster (page 101), one copy for display
- newspaper and magazine articles
- "Proofreading Marks" (page 104), one copy for display and one copy per student
- "Democracy in America" (page 103), one copy per student
- red pencils
- cardstock, 9" x 12" (23 cm x 30 cm), one sheet per student (optional)
- markers, rulers, and other art supplies (optional)

Preparation

Enlarge the "Conventions" poster (page 101) and "Proofreading Marks" (page 104) for display.

Opening

Share with the students the "Conventions" poster (page 101). Tell the students that the term *conventions* refers to "the rules of writing correctly." Authors who write effectively apply conventions to their writing so readers can understand what they have written.

Directions

1. Show the class the newspaper and magazine articles. Tell the students that editors use certain marks to show how to correct mistakes for final copy and publication. Editors call them proofreading marks.
2. Distribute copies of "Proofreading Marks" (page 104). Go over the marks with the students, demonstrating on the white board how to use each mark.
3. Distribute copies of "Democracy in America" (page 103). Tell the students that the article contains seven errors in spelling, capitals, punctuation, sentence structure, spacing, or paragraphs.
4. Have the students use red pencils to write proofreading marks on the article as applicable. Remind the students to read the article carefully; they may need to read through the article more than once.

Closing

Review editing changes made on page 103. Answer questions and explain the use of proofreading marks as necessary.

Extension

Have each student create a small poster to display the proofreading marks. Encourage the students to be creative. The design should not detract from this easy-to-use reference.

Democracy in America

by Issac F.

The United states has a democratic government. In type this of government, people elect officials to lead the country The Constitution calls this government "of the people, by the people, and for the people." The Citizens vote to elect a President. They also decide. Who will represent them in Congress. Generally, a majority vote wins. In this way, the concerns and interests of the people may be addressed by the leaders of the country.

Proofreading Marks

Mark	Explanation	Sample
⟲	delete word	remove the the word
∧	insert word	this needs go
#	insert space	add a spacehere
¶	paragraph break	¶ The final step is to add glue.
∧,	add comma	January 6, 2006
⊙	add period	That's the end⊙
?	add question mark	What would you like?
!	add exclamation point	Wow!
✕	misspelled word	Please cros this out.
≡	uppercase letter	montana
lc	lowercase letter	Compass

Following the Laws

Objective

Given a review of common rules for spelling, punctuation, and capitals, the students will edit a sample paragraph focusing on these aspects of the Conventions trait.

Materials

- "Proofreading Marks" (page 104)
- "The Process of Making a Law" (page 107), one copy per student
- colored pencils
- "Broken Rules" (page 106) (optional)
- "Catch the Culprit!" (page 108) (optional)
- cardstock, 9" x 12" (23 cm x 30 cm), three sheets (optional)

Preparation

Ensure that each student still has a copy of "Proofreading Marks" (page 104). If necessary, photocopy additional copies. Photocopy "Catch the Culprit!" (page 108) twice and photocopy "Broken Rules" (page 106) once onto cardstock; then cut the cards apart.

Opening

Direct the students' attention to the "Conventions" poster (page 101). Tell the class that they will focus on the second, third, and fourth conventions: spelling, capitalization, and punctuation.

Directions

1. Review high frequency spelling words and other words for which you hold your students responsible. Go over any strategies for checking spelling that your students have learned.

2. Ask the students to recall capitalization rules they have learned: capitalize proper names, titles of specific people, names of buildings, cities, states, countries, the first word of a sentence, etc.

3. Review rules of punctuation with the class, including the use of commas to separate clauses within sentences and offset names, transition words, and prepositional phrases; use of apostrophes, colons, and semicolons.

4. Distribute copies of "The Process of Making a Law" (page 107). Tell the students that the paragraph contains nine spelling, capitalization, or punctuation errors, which they will correct using proofreading marks. Have the students edit the paragraph with a colored pencil.

Closing

Ask the students to rewrite the paragraph correctly, based on the proofreading marks they made. As a class, go over the editing corrections.

Following the Laws *(cont.)*

Extension

Students will play a game in which they will "capture" people who have broken the law before they escape. Each student will receive one game card (page 108). The card will identify the role he or she will play in the game. Four people will be dealt a card with a mistake in spelling, capitalization, or punctuation (page 106). These people have "broken the law." They will try to escape the police by getting to one of four escape vehicles around the room. Four students will have been dealt an escape vehicle card, and they will need to make their presence known to help the criminals escape. Four additional students will receive a police card. They try to catch the offenders before they reach the escape vehicles. Four additional students will receive a rehabilitation center card; police may take a captured law breaker to these people where they will have the chance to rewrite the sentence correctly. The rest of the class will receive a bystander card; they may choose to help the police, help the law breakers escape, or be innocent bystanders. Have the two newspaper reporters comment on the progress of the game. The game is over when all four law breakers have completed rehabilitation (successfully corrected the sentences).

Broken Rules

the government protects people from harm.	Americas government has lasted for 200 years.
Are government has two major political parties.	The three branches of our government is the executive, legislative, and judicial.

The Process of Making a Law

by Bob P.

A "bill" is introduced debated and passed by the United States senate and House of Representatives. Then members of each House get together to ensure the bills have the same language. Once approved, the bill goes to the president. If he approves of the Bill, he signed it and the bill is now a law He then puts the presidential seal on the law.

Catch the Culprit!

police	police
escape vehicle	escape vehicle
rehabilitation center	rehabilitation center
bystander	bystander
bystander	bystander
bystander	newspaper reporter

Let's All Agree

Objective

Given a review of principles of grammar, the students will identify examples of specific principles and write a description using active verbs.

Materials

- white board, overhead projector, or chart paper and marker
- "Why Doesn't This Work?" (page 110), one copy for display
- scavenger hunt cards (page 112)
- "How Language Works" (page 113), one copy per pair
- cardstock, 9" x 12" (23 cm x 30 cm), one sheet
- "The Parts of Government Work Together" (page 111), one copy per student

Preparation

Enlarge "Why Doesn't This Work?" (page 110) for display. Prepare the scavenger hunt cards (page 112) by photocopying the page onto cardstock. Cut the page into strips. Place the strips around the classroom before beginning the lesson; you may wish to place them in obvious places or hide the cards from plain view.

Opening

Show the students pictures from "Why Doesn't This Work?" (page 110). Ask the students to identify what is not right about the pictures. Ask how they know it is not right. Explain that when we know how something is supposed to look, we know when it does not look right. Review the concept of a *diagram*, "a picture with labels that explains how something works." Tell the class that drawing a diagram can help them understand how something is supposed to work so they know when it is not working correctly. The same is true of language. Once students learn how language is supposed to work and how words go together correctly in sentences, they will find it easier to edit their writing; they will know when something doesn't look quite right.

Directions

1. Review concepts and rules of sentence structure and grammar such as subject-verb agreement, run-on sentences, sentence fragments, use of prepositional phrases, clauses, and word usage. Define and give one example of each. You may wish to take some time at this point to teach each principle, if necessary.

2. Tell the students they will go on a scavenger hunt to locate grammatical components of our language. Explain that an example of each principle has been printed on a card and placed around the room. When students find the card that matches a principle on their list, they should correctly write the words, phrase, or sentence and leave the card for other students.

Let's All Agree *(cont.)*

Directions *(cont.)*

3. Distribute copies of "How Language Works" (page 113). Divide the class into pairs. Students should begin at random places on their list to find the cards so that not everyone is in the same place at the same time during the scavenger hunt. Allow the students to move around the room, finding cards and writing the items they find on their paper.

Closing

Distribute copies of "The Parts of Government Work Together" (page 111). Have the students edit the sample for grammatical errors discussed in this lesson. (There are six errors.)

Extension

Have the groups prepare a skit, dramatizing what they know about how language works. Students may play the role of a part of speech, or the students may play the role of a teacher, explaining principles and concepts in a humorous way. Allow time for the students to present their skits to the class.

Why Doesn't This Work?

The Parts of Government Work Together

by Cindy L.

The government oversees matters of public concern in a city, state, or country. In the United States, the government consist of the president, Congress, and the Supreme Court. Each aspect of government has it's own duties. Congress takes charge of making laws the president signs or vetoes laws. When people break the law. The Supreme Court decides how to administer justice. All three branches of our government work together to oversee the country.

Scavenger Hunt Cards

House of Representatives and Senate

On the Fourth of July, America celebrates its independence.

The government make the laws for the country.

Before the Constitutional Convention, the colonies had the Articles of Confederation.

The president can suggest laws.

The president can sign a bill into law, but he cannot make laws.

If something happens too the president, the vice president becomes the president.

The people vote to choose a president to represent all the states the president serves four years in office until there is another election.

How Language Works

Find an example of each grammar principle below. Write the example next to the principle.

1. Run-on sentence:

   _____

   _____

2. Sentence fragment or incomplete sentence:

   _____

   _____

3. Subject-verb agreement:

   _____

   _____

4. Subject and verb do not agree:

   _____

   _____

5. Prepositional phrase:

   _____

   _____

6. Clauses joined by a comma:

   _____

   _____

7. Clauses joined with a conjunction:

   _____

   _____

8. Incorrect word usage:

   _____

   _____

Strong Words Make Strong Writing

Objective

Given instruction in passive and active voice, the students will identify passive voice in a sample and rewrite it using active voice.

Materials

- classroom resources on government topics
- student samples of active/passive voice
- "Simplify Gobbledygook" (page 115), one copy per student
- colored pencils, two different colors per student

Opening

Review with the students the "Conventions" poster (page 101). Ask the students what is meant by "use action verbs." Students may differentiate between words that show action, rather than thinking, feeling, or state of being verbs. Explain that *action verbs* may also refer to using "active voice" instead of "passive voice."

Directions

1. Continue a discussion on the concept of active voice compared to passive voice. Read student sample sentences from classroom resources that exhibit active and passive voice. Ask the students to identify the difference between the two types of sentences. Which one shows more energy and is more interesting to read? Explain that in passive voice, a subject is acted upon rather than actually doing the action. Model for the students how to change passive voice to active voice by removing any state of being verbs. Students should consider who or what is the subject of the sentence and what action the subject is doing. Tell the class that using strong action verbs will make their writing more effective.

2. Distribute copies of "Simplify Gobbledygook" (page 115). Have the students use a colored pencil to circle any state of being verbs or verb phrases written in passive voice. Students should use a different-colored pencil to circle any action verbs or phrases written in active voice. (There are four passive-voice sentences and four active-voice sentences.)

Closing

Have the students rewrite any phrases written in the passive voice using the active voice.

Extension

Invite the students to illustrate several action verbs to create a class book. Students may use stick figures that show action in a cartoon-style format, with or without color. They should write active-voice sentences to accompany their pictures. The class book may be used in the classroom library, school library, or given to a class of younger students.

Simplify Gobbledygook

by Rachel R.

The Constitution of the United States sets up the basic laws of our country.

People are protected by the Constitution so they may live in peace.

The first ten amendments of the Constitution are called the Bill of Rights.

The Bill of Rights gives people the freedom of speech and religion.

The Constitution was signed by members of the Constitutional Convention.

Our government has three branches: the executive branch, the legislative branch, and the judicial branch.

A new government was created by the delegates at the Constitutional Convention.

In America, the people elect leaders of the government.

It's All About Paragraphs

Objective

Given a review of the five-paragraph essay, the students will write questions, identify a problem or issue, and write an essay following this format.

Materials

- "How Students Can Make a Difference" (page 117), one copy per student
- "Thinking It Through" (page 118), one copy per student
- classroom resources about voting (optional)

Opening

Conduct a class discussion on voting. Show the class any election-related materials you may have. Ask the students what they know about voting and why it might be important to vote. Have the students consider who should and should not be allowed to vote and why they think this. Ask the students to think about whether or not anything should be changed about our current system of voting.

Directions

1. Refer the students to the "Conventions" poster (page 101) and tell them to check for appropriate paragraphs when they edit their writing. That is, they should make sure that each new idea or main point begins a new paragraph. If they have a few sentences about a topic, they should put all of those sentences together in one paragraph, rather than throughout their paper. This concept relates to the Organization trait—the students should organize their writing in a logical order and sequence. They will group their thoughts by topic or idea and place all sentences about one topic or subtopic together.

2. Distribute copies of "How Students Can Make a Difference" (page 117). You might want to read through the first four or five sentences together to demonstrate how to decide where to begin a new paragraph. Have the students read the remainder of the essay on their own, using the appropriate proofreading mark to indicate where each new paragraph should begin. If time allows, go over the paragraph divisions as a class. (There are five paragraphs.)

3. Distribute copies of "Thinking It Through" (page 118). Tell the students they will use this page to ask questions and identify a problem or issue related to voting or elections. They should also determine the main points and ideas, details, and examples they will include in their essay.

Closing

Have the students write an essay about an issue related to government, voting, or elections, using a five-paragraph essay format. Remind the students to check their work for appropriate paragraph divisions, as well as other aspects of the Conventions trait they have studied.

It's All About Paragraphs *(cont.)*

Extension

Group the students into teams representing two sides of an issue, based on similarity of student essay topics. For example, if several students wrote about who should and should not be allowed to vote, those students would be grouped into two teams, accordingly. Have the teams prepare statements and arguments for a debate. Once the teams have prepared, conduct the debates between teams. Establish the rules for debate before beginning: every person on a team should take a turn contributing to the debate; teams should take turns talking, posing arguments, questions, or responses; only one person should talk at a time; voices should be kept at a moderate indoor level.

How Students Can Make a Difference

by Jennifer T.

It may seem as if students' thoughts and opinions do not matter to adults. Students often feel they cannot change things they do not like. They wonder if they can do anything that will make a difference in their world. Students can make a difference if they decide to take action. An important first step is to have a plan. Students first need to decide what they would like to see changed. Then they should write any ideas they have for how things could be different. Once students have a plan, they can get organized. Being organized requires planning ahead. Students need to know what they will need to do to put their plan into action. They should think about any supplies, resources, or people needed to carry out the plan. Making a difference happens when others get involved. Students can ask peers, as well as adults, to help them with their plan. Students should be willing to listen to a grownup's suggestions, but it is good to ask the grownup to consider the student's ideas as well. Following these simple steps will help students act on ideas to change their community. As students see their plans and ideas in action, they will realize they can indeed make a difference.

Thinking It Through

Write three questions you would like to ask or answer about government, voting, or elections:

1. _____

2. _____

3. _____

What problems or issues do you see concerning our current government or system of voting or elections?

1. _____

2. _____

Write the main point of your essay:

_____

Write the three subtopics in your essay:

1. _____

2. _____

3. _____

What details or examples can you include for each subtopic?

1. _____

2. _____

3. _____

How will you conclude your essay? How will you refer back to the main point?

_____

Learning from Each Other

Objective

Given a review of the characteristics of the Conventions trait, the students will edit classmates' essays, and offer and apply feedback.

Materials

- white board, overhead projector, or chart paper and marker
- "Establish the Laws of Writing" (page 122), one copy per student
- student essays from "It's All About Paragraphs" (page 116), photocopied for student use
- "Proofreading Marks" (page 104)
- "How Students Can Make a Difference" (page 121), one copy for display
- colored pencils, eight different colors per student
- sticky notes, five per student

Preparation

Enlarge "How Students Can Make a Difference" (page 121) for display. Remove the names from the student essays so classmates can edit anonymously. Ensure that each student has a copy of "Proofreading Marks" (page 104). Make additional copies, if necessary.

Opening

Have the class conduct a student-led review of the characteristics of the Conventions trait. Have volunteers define, explain, and give examples of conventions students should watch for in their writing.

Directions

1. Explain that *criteria* refer to "rules or standards" by which writing may be evaluated. For example, the students may evaluate and edit their writing according to proper rules of spelling, capitalization, and punctuation.

2. Distribute copies of "Establish the Laws of Writing" (page 122). Have the students write one or two criteria for each aspect of the Conventions trait. Encourage the students to refer to the "Conventions" poster (page 101) or other reference materials to review various spelling and grammatical principles.

3. Tell the students they will use page 122, as well as other things they have learned about Conventions, to edit classmates' essays from the previous lesson. They should refer to "Proofreading Marks" (page 104) to show necessary editing changes.

Learning from Each Other *(cont.)*

Directions *(cont.)*

4. Divide the students into groups of five students each.

5. Have the students edit one classmate's essay for spelling, according to their checklist and other spelling rules they have learned. Each member of the group should use the same color pencil to edit for spelling.

6. Students will pass the papers to the person next to them. Everyone in the group will now edit for capitalization using a different colored pencil.

7. Have the students continue passing the papers around the group in this manner.

8. Show the students "How Students Can Make a Difference" (page 121). Read aloud the comments and feedback. Point out that even though the comments offer feedback on how to make the writing better, overall the person wrote positive comments. You might want to demonstrate writing positive comments and feedback as well.

9. Give each student five sticky notes. Students will pass the essay papers around the group once more. This time they should write at least one positive comment on a sticky note and place it on each classmate's essay. Students may also give positive feedback for improving the essay.

Closing

Have the students make changes to their essays, based on the feedback they have received. Ask the students to write a note at the bottom of the essay telling how the comments helped them.

Extension

Have each group prepare a simple lesson to teach younger students how to edit their work, based on the characteristics of the Conventions trait. Arrange a time for students to present their lessons to another class.

How Students Can Make a Difference

by Jennifer T.

Clearly demonstrates the five-paragraph essay.

It may seem as if students' thoughts and opinions do not matter to adults. Students often feel they cannot change things they do not like. They wonder if they can do anything that will make a difference in their world.

First paragraph is well constructed and clearly states thesis.

Students can make a difference if they decide to take action. An important first step is to have a plan. Students first need to decide what they would like to see changed. Then they should write any ideas they have for how things could be different.

Once students have a plan, they can get organized. Being organized requires planning ahead. Students need to know what they will need to do to put their plan into action. They should think about any supplies, resources, or people needed to carry out the plan.

Making a difference happens when others get involved. Students can ask peers, as well as adults, to help them with their plan. Students should be willing to listen to a grownup's suggestions, but it is good to ask the grownup to consider the student's ideas as well.

Good topic sentence for final paragraph. Provide a few ideas or examples for the reader in this paragraph.

Following these simple steps will help students act on ideas to change their community. As students see their plans and ideas in action, they will realize they can indeed make a difference.

Establish the Laws of Writing

Write two principles of spelling writers should remember: (for example, remember spelling rules for adding word endings)

☐ _____

☐ _____

Where will you check for capitals?

☐ _____

☐ _____

Write two punctuation rules you will watch for:

☐ _____

☐ _____

☐ Did the writer use any run-on sentences or sentence fragments?

☐ Does the essay have any words used incorrectly? (can/may, it's/its, etc.)

☐ Did the writer use action verbs? Are there places you can suggest active voice to take the place of passive voice?

☐ Does each main idea or subtopic have its own paragraph? Or should any paragraphs be combined into one paragraph because they are about the same thing?

☐ Does the essay have an appropriate title? Can you think of a better or more appropriate title?

Presentation

The trait of Presentation refers to the "publication" part of the writing process. After students have completed a written piece, they present it to their audience; visually, orally, or using both formats. The Presentation trait consists of two components: visual and auditory.

Students consider appropriate visual formats for their writing, as well as the use of color. Visual aids include charts, diagrams, graphs, and other ways of presenting information visually with or without text. Specifically, students learn how to create a diagram and note cards for a presentation.

The auditory component of Presentation includes presenting work in an oral format; students learn public speaking skills through drama and critique. Lessons also give students opportunity to practice speaking from personal experience and knowledge of a topic, to ask and respond to questions, and to state their main point clearly when presenting their writing to others.

Presentation

Visual Elements

- select a presentation format

- include illustrations that catch the reader's attention

- incorporate visual aids such as photos, drawings, charts, diagrams, and graphs

- express your own ideas and reflections

Auditory Elements

- tell about experience and knowledge of the topic

- ask and respond to questions

- have a clear main point when speaking to others

- read writing to others

- make eye contact while giving oral presentations

- organize your ideas for oral presentations (i.e., include content appropriate to the audience, use notes, summarize main points)

A Display for All to See

Objective

Given an introduction to the Presentation trait, the students will select a topic and begin to plan a presentation using visual and auditory components.

Materials

- overhead projector, transparencies, and marker
- "Presentation" poster (page 124), one copy for display
- "My Tiger Report" (page 127), one copy for display
- "Pleasing Pages" (page 128), one copy per student
- classroom resources about animal behavior
- presentation software (e.g., PowerPoint) (optional)
- computer projector (optional)

Preparation

Enlarge the "Presentation" poster (page 124) for display. Prepare "My Tiger Report" by enlarging each "slide" to fit on an 8 ½" x 11" (21.5 cm x 28 cm) overhead transparency. Color the background of each slide lightly: 1) blue, 2) red, 3) green, 4) yellow, 5) purple, 6) light gray speckled (other colors may be substituted as necessary). If you plan to have students use presentation software for the extension activity, you might want to re-create the sample using the software and display it on a computer screen or projector.

Opening

Show the students the "Presentation" poster (page 124). Point out the two aspects of Presentation: visual and auditory. Explain that when authors publish their writing, it must be presented in a way that catches the reader's attention. The *visual* component of Presentation refers to how writing looks, including how it is arranged on the page and any illustrations. The term *auditory* refers to presentations in which authors speak in front of other people. The writer may give a speech, present a report, or teach a lesson using his or her writing.

Directions

1. Show the students "My Tiger Report" (page 127), one slide at a time. Ask the students to observe the layout of text and pictures on each slide. How does the author use fonts and bullets? What makes the slides easy to read?

2. Discuss briefly with the students possible topics. Students will plan a complete presentation, which they will present during the final lesson in this unit. Many of the lessons will refer to animal behavior as a common theme; you might want your students to plan a project or report on an aspect of animal behavior that they have previously studied or to coincide with a current unit on animals.

A Display for All to See *(cont.)*

Directions *(cont.)*

3. Distribute copies of "Pleasing Pages" (page 128). Tell the students they will use this page to plan their presentation. Specifically, the students will focus on how they want to arrange text and pictures on each slide. Students can create individual pages even if presentation software is unavailable.

4. Have the students decide which subtopics or main points they will include in their presentation. They should also plan how each page will look.

Closing

Encourage the students to use classroom resources to gather information and take notes about their chosen topic. They may write their notes on page 128 or use additional pages as needed.

Extension

Students will need to complete the process of reading, researching, and taking notes on their topic before they will be able to participate in this activity. Have the students make a sample presentation using computer software. They should follow their plan as indicated on "Pleasing Pages" (page 128), creating five or six slides.

Monkeys

by Mckayla M.

My Tiger Report

1.

My Tiger Report

By:

Brianna K.

2. Animal Group

- Tigers are mammals.
- All mammals are warm-blooded.
- Tigers are vertebrates.
- Tigers are meat eaters.

3. Habitat

- Tigers like forests.
- The biggest tiger lives in Asia.
- Some tigers live together and some live alone.

4. Gathering Food

- A tiger hunts in long grass because the animals would see him if he hunted in short grass.
- The stripes help him blend into the grass.

5. Babies

- When tigers have babies, they have six of them.
- When babies are born, they drink their mom's milk.
- They are called cubs.

6.

That is the life of a tiger!

Pleasing Pages

1.

Title

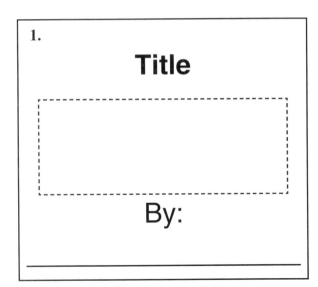

By:

_____

2.

_____

(heading)

• _____
• _____
• _____
• _____

3.

_____

(heading)

• _____
• _____
• _____
• _____

(list)

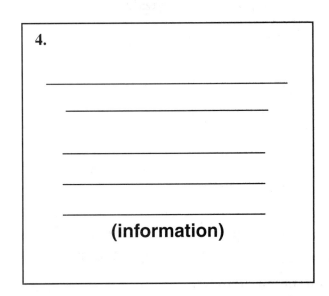

4.

_____

_____

_____

_____

(information)

5.

_____

(heading)

_____

6.

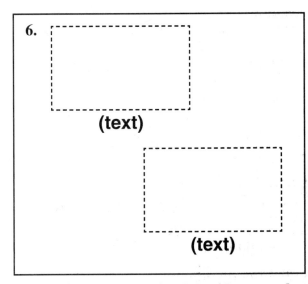

(text)

(text)

Preparing to Present

Objective

Given instruction on formats for presenting writing, the students will choose a format and submit a written proposal to the teacher.

Materials

- white board, overhead projector, or chart paper and marker
- "My Proposal" (page 130)
- "Many Forms of Writing" (pages 131–132), one copy per student
- puppets or craft supplies to make puppets: clean white socks or small paper bags, markers, fabric scraps, yarn (optional)

Preparation

If the students will be using puppets for the Extension activity and ready-made puppets are not available, you may have the students make their own puppets. Students may make puppets with clean white socks and felt tip markers. Draw the puppet's face on the foot of the sock and add other decorations as desired. Puppets may also be made from paper bags.

Opening

Ask the students to review what they have learned about page layouts. Direct the students' attention to the visual component on the "Presentation" poster (page 124). Explain that authors must sometimes choose the format they will use to present their writing. Tell the students that *format* refers to "the style of writing," or the way something is written or spoken.

Directions

1. Continue a class discussion on various formats authors may use to publish their writing. Have the students tell ways they have observed people share their work. Create a list on the white board.

2. Tell the students that authors may present writing in any of these ways:

   - give a speech that they have written
   - participate in an oral debate, for which they have prepared, taking notes and forming arguments
   - create a poster on which they write their ideas
   - take part in or lead a question-and-answer session on a selected topic
   - give a lecture or teach a lesson
   - write a skit for puppets

3. If necessary, explain any of the above presentation formats to your students.

Preparing to Present *(cont.)*

Directions *(cont.)*

4. Distribute copies of "Many Forms of Writing" (pages 131–132). Explain to the students that they will use this form to choose a format for their presentation. They will write a proposal to the teacher, indicating which format they will use to present their project.

5. Read aloud "My Proposal" (page 130). Discuss how the sample includes each aspect of planning addressed on the form. Ask the students whether or not the person chose the most appropriate way to present his or her topic and why.

6. Have the students complete "Many Forms of Writing" (pages 131–132). Students should refer to the same topic they chose in the previous lesson for their overall project.

Closing

Have the students write a summary paragraph on the back of page 132. Tell the students that this paragraph is their proposal, indicating what type of presentation they will give.

Extension

Divide the students into small groups. Have each group use puppets to tell the class about one part of the Presentation trait.

My Proposal

by Valencia M.

My presentation will be about penguins. I will ask my classmates to participate in a question-and-answer session. I chose this format because I think many people are interested in penguins and might have some questions about them. First, I will need to read some reference books and take notes about my topic. Then I will write some questions for the class to answer. I could also make a flip chart with questions on the outside flap and the answers printed inside. I will need a medium-sized piece of poster board, markers, some paper to put on the poster board to make flaps, and tape or glue to attach the flaps to the board. I think the students will enjoy my presentation; everybody seems to like penguins.

Many Forms of Writing

My topic is: _____

Choose the way you want to present your writing by checking the appropriate box:

☐ give a speech

☐ debate

☐ create a poster

☐ PowerPoint presentation

☐ question-and-answer session

☐ give a lecture

☐ teach a lesson

☐ write a puppet skit

Why did you choose this format?

_____

_____

_____

What information will you include in your presentation?

_____

_____

_____

Many Forms of Writing *(cont.)*

How will you organize what you want to say?

- Speech: Make an outline with introduction, three main points, details and examples, and conclusion.

- Debate: Read and prepare, take notes, form arguments, and write statements.

- Poster: How will you arrange text and graphics? Draw a rough draft, showing placement of your words and pictures.

- PowerPoint: How many slides will you have? What will be on each slide?

- Question and Answer: Write questions to ask, or write answers to questions you think the audience will ask.

- Lecture or Talk: Write an outline or notes with introduction, main points, details and examples, and conclusion.

- Teach a Lesson: What do you want the audience to know? How will you tell them?

- Drama: How many characters will you have? What will each character say? How will the characters discuss your topic?

What materials will you need to prepare your presentation, based on the format you chose?

Check the box of each material that applies.

- ☐ note cards
- ☐ poster board and markers
- ☐ time at a computer
- ☐ overhead projector and marker
- ☐ chart paper and marker
- ☐ pictures to show audience
- ☐ objects to make a point
- ☐ puppets
- ☐ puppet stage

Write a paragraph on the back of this page to your teacher, stating your choice of format for your presentation. Include the information you decided on from this page.

Displaying My Information

Objective

Given a review of forms of visual aids and instruction in making a chart, the students will create a chart about their chosen topic.

Materials

- white board, overhead projector, or chart paper and marker
- "How Animals Live" (page 134), one copy for display
- "Charting Animal Behavior" (page 135), one copy per student
- classroom resources on animal behavior
- computers with spreadsheet software capable of creating tables, graphs, and other types of charts (optional)

Preparation

Enlarge "How Animals Live" (page 134) for display.

Opening

Review the oral writing formats speakers may use to present their writing as discussed in "Preparing to Present" (page 129). Tell the students that sometimes it is easier to understand and remember something when they can see a picture, diagram, chart, or graph.

Directions

1. Explain that the items listed above are *visual aids*, or something people look at to help them understand the message of a presentation. Discuss how and why visual aids can help the audience understand an author's writing.

2. Show the students "How Animals Live" (page 134). Tell them that charts may include maps, graphs, tables, or diagrams. Explain that this chart is in the form of a table, which displays different categories of information in relationship to each other. Point out various aspects of the table.

3. Continue to refer to "How Animals Live" (page 134). Use the white board to model how to create a simple table. A table has columns and rows, often with a specific heading for each column. A table may provide general information in the form of an overview about a topic or it may display details.

4. Distribute copies of "Charting Animal Behavior" (page 135). Tell the students to focus on the topic of their presentation as they create the table. They will use classroom resources, as well as any notes they have, to create a table. They may need to share information with other students in order to create a table with comparison data.

5. Have the students use page 135 to create a simple table. Monitor the students as they work, assisting them as necessary.

Displaying My Information *(cont.)*

Closing

Have the students share their tables with the class. Classmates may ask questions for clarification.

Extension

Have the students enter their data into a computer program that will guide them through creating a table or graph. You may have to give brief instruction regarding where on the menu to find various commands. For example, from Microsoft® Word, a student can go to "Table, Insert, Table" to find a screen indicating how many columns and rows to create in a table. Students may also use the "Insert, Picture, Chart" series of commands to enter data and then select a type of graph to create.

How Animals Live

Name of Animal	What It Eats	When It Sleeps	How It Gathers Food	Habitat
owl	mice, squirrels	during the day	hunts prey	trees
grizzly bear	fish, small mammals	nighttime	hunts prey	den or cave, dense forest, Northwest, United States
koala	eucalyptus leaves	during the day	gathers food from trees; picks leaves	trees, Australia
squirrel	seeds, nuts, berries	nighttime	gathers seeds, nuts, berries; stores food for winter	light forests, dense forests, all over the world
rabbit	grass, leaves, berries	nighttime	gathers berries; grazes on grass	briar patches, bushes, light forests, edge of forests

Charting Animal Behavior

Final Stages of Planning

Objective

Given a review of the characteristics of the Presentation trait and techniques of questioning, the students will complete a project planning sheet and write a presentation outline.

Materials

- white board, overhead projector, or chart paper and different colored markers
- "My Presentation Outline" (page 138), one copy for display
- "Project Planner" (page 139), one copy per student
- copies of student work from previous lessons, specifically "Pleasing Pages" (page 128) and "Many Forms of Writing" (pages 131–132)
- magazine pictures related to animal behavior
- index cards, one per student

Preparation

Enlarge "My Presentation Outline" (page 138) for display. Prepare the question cards by writing one large question mark on each index card, one per student.

Opening

Focus the students' attention on the "Presentation" poster (page 124). Review all aspects of the trait: visual and auditory. Tell the students they will need to think about these characteristics as they plan their actual presentation.

Directions

1. Tell the students that an important part of planning their presentation will be thinking about what they want to say. When they write something on paper, they include their own ideas and reflections. The same will be true for presenting their writing orally. Just as written pieces include personal experience and knowledge of the topic, they will also want to express their knowledge and experience when they speak to others. Effective writing is organized so as to not lose a reader; oral speaking will need to be that much more organized so as to not lose a listener. They should have a clear main point when speaking and presenting their thoughts aloud.

2. You may want to focus specifically on the final characteristic of Presentation, listing for your students the specific aspects related to organizing a presentation: content appropriate for audience, use of notes or other memory aids, and summary of main points.

3. Show the class "My Presentation Outline" (page 138). Explain that this student wrote some notes in planning a presentation but did not specify how his or her plan incorporated all necessary aspects of the Presentation trait.

Final Stages of Planning *(cont.)*

Directions *(cont.)*

4. Distribute copies of "Project Planner" (page 139). Review each item listed on the page, referring back to previous lessons as necessary. Tell the students they will use this outline to evaluate "My Presentation Outline" (page 138) as a class.

5. Ask the students to identify each component listed on "Project Planner" (page 139) in regard to page 138. For example, the students should identify the sentence(s) in the sample that refers to which format the student chose to use for Presentation. Use different colored markers to highlight each item on page 138.

Closing

Have the students use "Project Planner" (page 139) to finalize plans for their presentation. Tell the students they should use any notes and charts they have already composed, as well as the ideas they wrote on their proposal and forms from previous lessons. If necessary, distribute copies of student work that you have gathered (see Materials section).

Extension

Tell the students that the oral component of Presentation often includes responding to questions posed by an audience; the students should learn how to concisely answer questions. Distribute question cards to the students. Display the pictures related to student topics for presentations. Ask the students to think of questions they could ask about the pictures. When they think of a question, they should hold up their question card. Call on volunteers to ask questions. Other students may answer questions as appropriate. You might want to designate one or two students to act as scribes and write on the white board the questions students ask. Have the students discuss the types of questions asked by classmates. Discuss questioning techniques: inquiring, asking rhetorical questions, asking a leading question, presenting a problem, seeking, querying, interviewing, challenging as in a quiz, and raising a question for consideration and thought.

My Presentation Outline
by Oscar S.

I will present my project with a PowerPoint presentation. The presentation will have five slides. I can include my photographs from the zoo on the slides. One of the slides will have a chart that shows different types of bears and where they live. My topic is bears, which is appropriate for my audience because we study about animals in our class. I will not include too much information because I think the audience will pay better attention if I give a short presentation. I will have note cards to help me as I talk in case I cannot clearly see the PowerPoint presentation from where I have to stand. I could ask the audience for questions at the end and respond to their questions.

Type of bear	Eating	Sleeping	Habitat
	uuu uuu uu uuu uuu. uu uuuu uu uu uuuu uuu	*uuu uuu uu uuu uuu. uu uuuu uu uu uuuu uuu*	*uuu uuu uu uuu uuu. uu uuuu uu uu uuuu uuu*
	uuu uuu uu uuu uuu. uu uuuu uu uu uuuu uuu	*uuu uuu uu uuu uuu. uu uuuu uu uu uuuu uuu*	*uuu uuu uu uuu uuu. uu uuuu uu uu uuuu uuu*
	uuu uuu uu uuu uuu. uu uuuu uu uu uuuu uuu	*uuu uuu uu uuu uuu. uu uuuu uu uu uuuu uuu*	*uuu uuu uu uuu uuu. uu uuuu uu uu uuuu uuu*

Project Planner

1. I chose this format for my presentation:

   _____

   _____

2. My project includes this type of illustration:

   _____

   _____

3. I will use this kind of visual aid:

   _____

   _____

4. My notes or memory aids I will use to help me when I talk:

   _____

   _____

5. To introduce my project, I will say . . .

   _____

   _____

6. My main points:

   _____

   _____

7. My personal experience or knowledge about this topic:

   _____

   _____

8. What I say will be appropriate for my audience because . . .

   _____

   _____

9. I think the audience may ask these questions:

   _____

   _____

10. I can respond to their questions by . . .

    _____

    _____

My Presentation

Objective

Given a review of public speaking skills, each student will make a final presentation of his or her project to the class.

Materials

- "Speaking Clearly" (below), one copy for display
- "Listening to My Classmates" (page 141), one copy per student; multiple copies per student (optional)
- guest speaker (optional)

Preparation

Enlarge "Speaking Clearly" (page 140) for display.

Opening

Have the students review the visual and auditory components on the "Presentation Poster" (page 124). Ask the students why it is important to learn to present their writing to others.

Directions

1. Show the class "Speaking Clearly" (below). Have the students identify the correct public speaking actions. Ask the students why some actions (e.g., talking too fast or quietly) would not be appropriate when speaking to a group.
2. Distribute copies of "Listening to My Classmates" (page 141). Review the critique form with the class, ensuring that the students understand each item.

Closing

Allow time for the students to present their projects to the class. Have the students evaluate one or more classmates using page 141. Students should write at least one positive comment at the bottom of the page.

Extension

Invite a guest speaker to come to the class and talk about making presentations in front of a group. Or, have the guest speaker discuss a topic of current study. Prior to the presentation to the class, ask the guest's permission for students to evaluate his or her public speaking skills.

Speaking Clearly

Listening to My Classmates

Give the speaker a score that indicates how well you could understand his or her presentation. Circle the appropriate number. Use 1 to indicate the speaker did not exhibit this public speaking skill much at all and 5 to indicate excellence. At the bottom of the page, write a few positive comments to the speaker.

Eye contact: Did the speaker look at the audience?

1   2   3   4   5

Rate: Did the speaker talk too fast or too slow?

1   2   3   4   5

Volume: Did the speaker talk too loudly or too quietly?

1   2   3   4   5

Organization: Did the speaker have a clear main point?

1   2   3   4   5

Did the speaker use notes?

1   2   3   4   5

Did the speaker read from a paper or know what to say?

1   2   3   4   5

Content: Was the topic and style appropriate for the audience?

1   2   3   4   5

Audience: Did you pay attention and listen respectfully?

1   2   3   4   5

Comments: _____

_____

Technology Resources

American Folklore

http://www.americanfolklore.net

American folklore stories by type, state, or character. Provides brief synopsis and text of stories.

edHelper.com

http://www.edhelper.com

General reference site for lesson plans and resources for teachers. Includes printable reproducible activity pages in all subject areas.

Education Resource Information Center

http://www.eric.ed.gov

Database of educational journal articles. Search using "writing traits" or "6+1 Trait writing." Or search by document #ED481235 or #ED485670 for specific articles with an overview of 6+1 Trait™ writing.

The Educator's Reference Desk

http://www.eduref.org

General teaching reference site. Includes articles, resources, links, and lesson plans for all subject areas.

GEM: Gateway to 21st Century Skills

http://www.thegateway.org

General education resource site. Click on "First Time Users" button to learn how to navigate the site. Includes information on content areas.

Kent (Washington) School District

http://www.kent.k12.wa.us

Click on "Curriculum" on the left sidebar. Then click on "more," then "writing." A wealth of resources on 6+1 Trait™ writing, including an overview chart of the traits, lesson plans, and assessment. Includes resources for other content areas sorted by grade level.

The Northwest Regional Educational Laboratory

http://www.nwrel.org

The "parent" of 6+1 Trait™ writing; researchers first identified and defined effective writing traits at this regional educational laboratory. Offers definitions of the traits, trait prompts, tips for teachers, lesson plans, and assessment scoring guides.

TeachersFirst.com

http://www.teachersfirst.com

Overall resource site for teachers. Offers content matrix to search lesson plans in various subject areas.

Teachers Net

http://www.teachers.net

General reference site, specifically for lesson plans. Click on lesson plans on the home page, then on subject area. Lessons sorted by general subject area or grade levels only.

Web English Teacher

http://www.webenglishteacher.com

Click on "Writing" on the left sidebar to find articles, lesson plans, and assessment resources for using 6+1 Trait™ writing in the classroom.

Writing Fix

http://www.writingfix.com

Click on "6+1 Traits" on the left sidebar for a variety of helpful resources.

General Search Engines

To search a general search engine, such as *http://www.google.com*, use key phrase "6+1 Trait writing" to retrieve several links.

Answer Key

Page 103 (corrections are boldfaced)

The United **States** has a democratic government. In **this** type of government, people elect officials to lead the **country**. The Constitution calls this government "of the people, by the people, and for the people." The **citizens** vote to elect a **president**. They also **decide who** will represent them in Congress. Generally, a majority vote wins. In this way, the concerns and interests of the people may be addressed by the leaders of the country.

Page 107 (corrections are boldfaced)

A "bill" is **introduced**, **debated,** and passed by the United States **Senate** and House of Representatives. Then members of each **house** get together to ensure the **bill has** the same language. Once approved, the bill goes to the president. If he approves of the **bill**, he **signs** it and the bill is now a **law.** He then puts the presidential seal on the law.

Page 111 (corrections are boldfaced)

The government oversees matters of public concern in a city, state, or country. In the United States, the government **consists** of the president, Congress, and the Supreme Court. Each aspect of government has **its** own duties. Congress takes charge of making **laws**. **The** president signs or vetoes laws. When people break the **law**, **the** Supreme Court decides how to administer justice. All three branches of our government work together to oversee the country.

Page 113

1. The people vote to choose a president to represent all the states the president serves four years in office until there is another election. (run-on sentence)

2. House of Representatives and Senate (sentence fragment or incomplete sentence)

3. The president can suggest laws. (subject-verb agreement)

4. The government make the laws for the country. (subject and verb do not agree)

5. On the Fourth of July, America celebrates its independence. (prepositional phrase)

6. Before the Constitutional Convention, the colonies had the Articles of Confederation. (clauses joined by a comma)

7. The president can sign a bill into law, but he cannot make laws. (clauses joined with a conjunction)

8. If something happens too the president, the vice president becomes the president. (incorrect word usage of *too*)

Answer Key (cont.)

Page 115

The Constitution of the United States sets up the basic laws of our country. (active)

People are protected by the Constitution so they may live in peace. (passive)

Rewrite: The Constitution protects people so they may live in peace.

The first ten amendments of the Constitution are called the Bill of Rights. (passive)

Rewrite: The Bill of Rights forms the first ten amendments of the Constitution.

The Bill of Rights gives people the freedom of speech and religion. (active)

The Constitution was signed by members of the Constitutional Convention. (passive)

Rewrite: Members of the Constitutional Convention signed the Constitution.

Our government has three branches: the executive branch, the legislative branch, and the judicial branch. (active)

A new government was created by the delegates at the Constitutional Convention. (passive)

Rewrite: The delegates created a new government at the Constitutional Convention.

In America, the people elect leaders of the government. (active)

Page 117

¶It may seem as if students' thoughts and opinions do not matter to adults. Students often feel they cannot change things they do not like. They wonder if they can do anything that will make a difference in their world.

¶Students can make a difference if they decide to take action. An important first step is to have a plan. Students first need to decide what they would like to see changed. Then they should write any ideas they have for how things could be different.

¶Once students have a plan, they can get organized. Being organized requires planning ahead. Students need to know what they will need to do to put their plan into action. They should think about any supplies, resources, or people needed to carry out the plan.

¶Making a difference happens when others get involved. Students can ask peers, as well as adults, to help them with their plan. Students should be willing to listen to a grownup's suggestions, but it is good to ask the grownup to consider the student's ideas as well.

¶Following these simple steps will help students act on ideas to change their community. As students see their plans and ideas in action, they will realize they can indeed make a difference.